MEET "MRS. X"

"I *do* love my husband . . . in my own way. But the simple truth is that although my husband's a good guy —the salt of the earth—I find him and our marriage BORING AS HELL! All we share, after many years of marriage, is our love for the children and a strong physical attraction."

Sound familiar? If it does, you may be ready for THE ADULTERY GAME, the #1 Sensuous Alternative to the "Bored Housewife Syndrome." Here's how "Mrs. X" found a whole new world of excitement and satisfaction—while preserving the harmony of her home. "Mrs. X" includes a wealth of experienced advice on every aspect of THE ADULTERY GAME . . . from Finding a Playmate (even if you're a "boxed-in housewife" it *can* be done!) to Making Your Exit (a host of fabulous excuses for getting out of the house, even at the oddest hours) to What Playmates Want (everything you'll need to know—in bed and out) and much, much more!

> "I certainly would have tried to write this book, if I had known there was a publisher with the guts to publish it. It's a *must* for all would-be adulteresses and lots of fun for those who won't, don't, or can't!"
>
> PAMELA MASON, star of radio, TV, and screen and Columnist for the new national magazine, *Feminine Fitness*

THE
ADULTERY GAME

"Mrs. X"

PYRAMID BOOKS   ▲   NEW YORK

This book is dedicated to all Playmates, never to be forgotten, but especially to H.H. and J.S.

All names, places, etc. have been changed—for obvious reasons!

THE ADULTERY GAME
A PYRAMID BOOK

Copyright © 1973 by Stonehill Publishing Company, a division of Stonehill Communications, Inc.

Pyramid edition published January 1975

ISBN 0-515-03582-3

Printed in the United States of America

Pyramid Books are published by Pyramid Communications, Inc. Its trademarks, consisting of the word "Pyramid" and the portrayal of a pyramid, are registered in the United States Patent Office.

Pyramid Communications, Inc., 919 Third Avenue, New York, N.Y. 10022

ACKNOWLEDGMENTS

All of the information contained within represents, in addition to the experiences, views and opinions of Mrs. X., the observations and thoughts of friends, both male and female, who in their own special ways have contributed to making this book possible.

Most grateful thanks to Page Cuddy without whose interest this book would never have become a reality.

CONTENTS

7

THE
ADULTERY GAME

THE GAME

I am an ADULTERESS.

I've been playing for years, yet my husband, even my closest friends don't suspect my game. "Impossible," you say? Read on.

I wouldn't be surprised if some of your dearest friends, "good" women you've known for years, are playing "The Game" right now. For most of you this book will be an eye-opener, because personal adultery experiences are *rarely* discussed openly. Would you admit to a secret life? Could you?

I'm going to "tell it like it is." Every word in this book is true, every experience real. I spare no details, pull no punches. It's all here, everything you need to know—who, when, where, why and *how*. Once you've learned the rules and they're vital, you can begin the exhilarating experience of playing "The Game."

What are we like—we who are playing "The Game?" Not much different from you. First and foremost, we are wives and mothers. We are not thrill-seeking nymphomaniacs who seduce every man we meet. And yet the word "adulteress" conjures up just such exotic images. The wives of unfaithful husbands are especially guilty of this misconception. The "other woman" is a "whore," a "slut," or a "tramp," to use just a few of the more popular names. This book, once and for all, dispels those myths; I guarantee that!

13

Can you recognize "us"? Not by physical appearance, that's for sure! We are not all fantastically built, ravishing seductresses. In fact, we look and dress quite like you. But there *is* something different about "us." A look of fulfillment, joy. We are average American middle-aged housewives. And we live a secret life. We stay married. And we play "The Game."

The game is ADULTERY.

1

WHY WE STAY...

In the words of our former President, let me make one thing perfectly clear. I am one hundred percent in favor of mutually satisfying marriage. Nevertheless, it is a cold, hard fact of life that the divorce rate is at an all-time high. In the U.S., roughly one out of every four marriages ends in divorce or annulment. Each year divorce disrupts the lives of about 1,300,000 men, women and children.

Do *you* honestly consider yourself *happily* married? Or would you contemplate divorce if you were in a position to do so? I thought so. Like so many dissatisfied couples you've probably stayed married for the standard reasons, the common excuses.

Here are some of the most popular:

"The Children"

Many couples "stick it out" because they feel that children *need* both parents. Many are concerned about the psychological impact. They feel that their children, after all, didn't *ask* to be born, and it's their *duty* to remain together. But, when the children leave the nest, do "Mom" and "Dad" get a divorce? Not very often!

"Our Religion"

Deep religious convictions often keep a shaky marriage intact. Most religions forbid divorce—many on pain of expulsion from the church. But adultery, being only a "sin," is consequentially pardonable. Thus, it seems to me, most religions actually "prefer" adultery to divorce. But, what do you think?

"Money, Money, Money, Money, Money . . ."

Let's face it; ending a marriage can be *expensive*. Community property—the house and furnishings, maybe even the family business—have to be divided equally. That can cost plenty. Not to mention alimony and/or child support.

Many unhappy wives will "hang in" (put up with an unsatisfactory marriage) because they're not sure they can earn a living. Some wives don't want to work. They stick it out for economic security: a home of their own, a husband's paycheck, *his* health insurance, *his* retirement benefits, etc. They know on which side their bread is buttered and they're not about to give that up.

"Status"

If *I* were a sales clerk who married a member of the "jet set," *I'd* stay married too! Who wouldn't? Wives of top businessmen, doctors, lawyers, men in public office, etc., often stay married just for the status that their prominent husbands give them. Often, too, wives of rich and important men *enjoy* their lives: winter cruises, unlimited charge accounts at the best shops, summers in the South of France, private schools for the kids, country clubs, etc. It doesn't sound too bad, does it?

* * *

What's *your* excuse? Are you staying married for any or all of these reasons, or others like them? If so, welcome to the club. Only a small minority of married couples find physical, emotional, and intellectual fulfillment together. The high divorce rate proves that! What is the solution? For me, it's simple—I play "The Game" as an *alternative* to divorce.

The fact is, love was not always considered a prerequisite for marriage. Adulterous *liaisons* were once socially acceptable. Today, however, divorce is the norm. This has resulted in the rapid disintegration of the family unit, leaving millions of children (who are helpless to do anything about it) heartbroken and confused. Adultery is taboo, while divorce (with its frequently dire consequences) is condoned! Perhaps the Sixth Commandment should be "THOU SHALT NOT COMMIT DIVORCE."

Adultery can actually make a marriage work.

Hard to believe? Before reaching any conclusions, hear me out. That's all I ask.

Let's start with what I know best—me. I'm over thirty, a wife, a mother and homemaker. I live in an average neighborhood in a medium-size city where I can still walk my dog at night in relative safety. My house is clean, if at times a bit cluttered. I cook well, and my family does *not* live on TV dinners! I belong to the PTA and, once a year, can be counted on to bake my special "Yum Yum" cake for the school's baked goods sale; or to whip up a few dozen cookies —with only a couple of hours' notice—for the Boy Scouts, the Brownies, or a kindergarten party. I'm the first to offer my services if a neighbor's child is sick or a friend is in the hospital. My domestic talents are numerous: from knitting hats and mittens to growing African violets or "tie-dying" my son's jeans. I've decorated my home on "peanuts" (by purchasing used furniture and refinishing it myself), and I can create gourmet meals from hamburger. I can stretch a dollar like rubber . . . just a typical American housewife. Who washes 30,000 dishes a year. UGH!

I am also prolific. My house is full of children of varying ages and sexes. My most serious responsibility is being a mother; that's *why* I stay married. Because in addition to food, clothing and shelter, children require limitless love, understanding, encouragement, patience and discipline from *two* parents who love them.

My children are normal children, probably much like yours. At times they're noisy, silly, affectionate, dirty, demanding, angry, frightened, adorable, messy and deaf (to my requests to take out the garbage). And sometimes they're a pain in the neck. But I love them, and I'd gladly give my life (and maybe I have) for them.

I am also aware that they are not merely extensions of myself, of *my* hopes and dreams. They are individuals. They have a right to "do their own thing." I must allow them to mature, break away, as I know they must, when the time comes. I always try to remember that child care is only a temporary job.

By society's standards and to all outward appearances, my marriage is perfect. I *do* love my husband . . . in my own way. He is a dependable provider, an exceptionally patient and affectionate father who loves our children deeply. He's also a versatile and considerate lover and quite attractive, too, in his own way.

But with all this I was miserable. *Miserable?* How could anyone who has everything be *miserable*, you ask? I can only answer for myself, and for me the simple truth is that although my husband's a good guy

—the salt of the earth—I find him *and* our marriage BORING AS HELL! All we share, after many years of marriage, is our love for the children and a strong physical attraction.

Does this sound familiar, gals?

* * *

And what about those of you *who do not have sexual compatibility?* Has sex, for you, become just humdrum? Or *worse?* This doesn't necessarily mean that your husband isn't a "stud"—just that he no longer turns *you* on. Bored in bed, a wife may appear frigid, yet this same woman may be a *wild and abandoned tigress* with her Playmate. A change of partner and . . . Voilà! Her frigidity is cured!

What shape is *your* marriage in?

Older women with grown children and secure jobs often feel that it is no longer necessary to submit passively to their husbands' sexual demands. They are bored, sexually, emotionally, and often intellectually, with their mates. You might well ask:

Why stay married?

Why live with a man you don't have sex with, no longer love and are unhappy with?

Many times these women realize, and have had the experience to know that the grass is not always as green as it looks on the other side. How many over-40 divorced women have *you* known who were really better off? Was it the pot of gold at the end of the rainbow? Or the bottom of the barrel?

Youth acts impulsively; the mature person thinks first. Divorce is final—once done; you walk alone, live alone, face *all* your problems ALONE. Are *you* really prepared for that, prepared to maintain your own home, car, budget, insurance, taxes, your own job? And what if you become ill or disabled and can't support yourself? After a divorce, there's *no one* to help or care. Among other things, a husband is a bulwark against the often harsh, practical demands of life.

That's why for many women playing "The Game" can be a wonderful alternative: an exciting new existence, without the finality or risk of divorce. But it's a decision you must make for yourself. As for *me*, I've made mine. I play "The Game"—but always by the rules.

2

... AND WHY WE PLAY

Playing "The Game" lets you have your cake *and* eat it too. You *can* have the best of both! But you've got to know what you're doing!

If I choose divorce, I stand to lose more than I gain. My children would be deprived of the father they dearly love, and economic security, as well. I'd get my "freedom"—but at what cost? And what kind of freedom? For me, marriage is the lesser of two evils. Instead of getting divorced, I play "The Game." And that's exactly what it should be: A GAME!

According to *Webster's Dictionary,* a game is "a sport or diversion." You might say then that "The Game" is my *hobby.* Instead of bowling with the girls every Wednesday night, or belonging to the neighborhood sewing circle, I play a different game. A game that takes only a few hours a week. A game that I find more interesting, more fun and more rewarding than any other. I spend four hours a week on my favorite hobby; the other one hundred sixty-four hours I'm wife, mother, cook, nurse, and maid, in addition to occasional outside employment. And those few hours a week make all the difference in the world!

Several of my friends play "The Game." Each has her own reasons.

The Dumb Wife

Betty's domestic scene is typical of many, maybe even yours. Married right after high school, she is now in her mid-thirties and has two kids. Her college-grad husband considers Betty "below" him intellectually. Betty felt so inferior to this "genius" that she compensated by eating compulsively. At thirty, she weighed one hundred eighty pounds. Being home all day, she got fatter and fatter, while her husband worked his way up the proverbial ladder, leaving Betty far behind ... or so he thought!

But then the worm turned: Betty started dieting, exercising, reading. Gradually she got herself back in shape, physically and intellectually. *In less than six months she was a new woman.* But her husband had taken her for granted so long, he didn't even notice. Or *care!* Because of her husband's indifference, Betty now has her own secret life. Adultery brought vitality to her existence.

The Dependent Husband

Then there's Louisa, married to a guy who can't even tie his shoe laces without her. Now that the children have reached their teens, she's taken a full-time job ... in addition to playing "The Game." Several years ago she became fed up with her husband's complete dependence. He's like a clinging child. He has no hobbies, *nothing* but her! The poor girl was being smothered by her husband's dependence. Adultery offers her a chance to find the normal male-female relationships missing in her marriage.

The Odd Couple

Annette is married to a guy who's really fantastic —except for one slight problem: he's bi-sexual! He's VP of a large manufacturing company and they live in an expensive, twelve-room house. They have a full-time housekeeper and go to Europe at least once a year. And, they do have children. But her husband refuses to give up the boyfriend he's had for years.

Imagine Annette's shock when she returned home unexpectedly one evening and discovered her husband and his boyfriend making love in *her* bed, the boyfriend wearing *her* nightie! She swears her husband satisfies her sexually, but now she, too, plays "The Game." And it's not hard to see why!

The Forced Marriage

We all know couples who have married because of pregnancy. "I-had-to" marriages often push a wife (or husband) into playing "The Game." In this situation sometimes divorce *is* the only solution.

A young woman I know, Cora, took the forced marriage route for moral reasons. Her marriage hung together for three years. Although her husband pursued his own interests he felt trapped, tied down, thwarted. So Cora played "The Game," until she faced facts and walked out while still young enough to make a new life for herself.

The Male Chauvinist

Another couple, Frederick and Emily, would have divorced years ago, if not for five children . . . *and* the fact that Emily plays "The Game." Frederick, the typical Archie Bunker-type male chauvinist, honestly believes that housewives have it made. He tells Emily: "I earn the money—I decide how it's spent!" And: "A woman's place is in the home, the kitchen and the bedroom." Adultery literally saved Emily's sanity! And her marriage!

The Under-sexed Husband

Max and Jane's problem is typical of many marriages. After the "glow" wore off, Max let himself go. He now weighs two hundred pounds, is partially impotent, and has substituted food for sex. Jane, on the other hand, is vibrant, attractive and sexually alive. Making love once a month (which is all Max can handle) wasn't nearly enough for Jane. Until *she* learned to play "The Game!"

* * *

Remember, divorce is not the *only* solution to an unhappy marriage. Playing "The Game" helps. A secret affair adds new dimension to your life. Your husband and children *are* an important part of your world, but not your whole world. Through playing "The Game," you meet interesting people from all walks of life, you experience new and exciting points of view, philosophies, ideas. Every new man teaches you something. Every experience adds to your life, your knowledge and understanding, in some way.

Once you start playing "The Game" you'll find yourself a changed wife, nicer, more fun to be with and around. To cover up your tracks, you try harder. You speed through boring chores. Being a fuller woman (rather than one who's yearning), you give your best to your "regular" life. A happier, more fulfilled woman makes a better wife and mother.

Always remember, it's not *how much* time you give, but *what you are* when you give it. When I'm having an affair with someone I genuinely like and admire, I bring my happiness home. The morning after, even the most tedious chores are bearable. Washing breakfast dishes, I relive the events of the night before when I was "Queen-For-A-Night." My exciting double life relieves the monotony of day-to-day living.

True, playing "The Game" *is* escapism. It's one of the best methods of escapism I've found. And I've tried *almost* everything!

Warning!

Face facts: your marriage should end IMMEDIATELY if:

1. You are married to an alcoholic who beats you and abuses the children.
2. A compulsive gambler, who loses his week's salary . . . if he works at all!
3. A sexual pervert.
4. A perpetual playboy who ignores his financial and emotional obligations as father and husband.
5. A sadist who ties you to the bed and beats you (unless this is your bag, too).
6. A masochist.

Playing "The Game" won't solve any of these problems! In these cases I'd say that divorce is the answer. For your sake and for the safety of the children.

3

THE BORED HOUSEWIFE
SYNDROME

After years of observation and endless "girl talk," I can state unequivocally that *almost all housewives are victims of "The Bored Housewife Syndrome."* They are isolated from the mainstream of life and bound by monotonous work, day after day, year in and year out. Washing dishes, cooking meals, mopping floors, sorting laundry, and ironing *are* necessary duties that must be done by someone. But it's boring just the same.

The only advantage is complete protection from the cold-hearted business world, its pressures and tensions. A housewife sets her own schedule; she is her own boss. No one stands over her eight hours a day telling her what to do and how. Nor is she expected to make decisions on which thousands of dollars ride.

My friends (as they get older) sometimes ask: "Where am I after all these years of marriage?" Their husbands are married to their jobs. Their almost-grown children check in every once-in-a-while for a change of clothes or a meal. But they have their own worlds. They no longer keep her busy. Occasionally, Mother is needed for advice or discipline, but that's it. Home alone for at least eight hours a day, the time drags on. Now what? Where does she go from here? With no young children to tie her down, what's her excuse for not developing her potential?

The mother whose young children are still completely dependent on her is in a very different position. She is kept *too* busy. There just aren't enough hours in the day to get all her work done. Her life is like the old adage: "A man works from sun to sun, but a woman's work is never done." The young mother needs diversion, not divorce. For her, marriage is an economic necessity, yet because of the monotony of her daily routine, she feels like she's on a treadmill, the same boring tasks over and over again, no end in sight, and no pay check, either.

What would it cost to replace her? If she were employed as a professional housekeeper and worked only eight hours a day in someone else's house, she would receive a decent salary, an hour for lunch, time-and-a-half for overtime, two weeks paid vacation and social security. And did you realize that a woman who has never been employed cannot collect social security when she reaches the age of sixty-five? No wonder the housewife who is completely tied down at home sometimes feels tired, depressed and bored.

What is the answer for her?

There are a great number of easy quick escape routes from the loneliness of those four walls. Many women are avid readers of everything from bestsellers to the *Reader's Digest*. Others watch TV, hours of "soaps" or game shows. Some gals chat on the phone or coffee clatch for hours with friends. Some are fanatical housekeepers. (We all know one of these "Mrs. Cleans." She finds fulfillment in the endless cleaning and polishing of her private domain.)

While these methods do help alleviate boredom, they leave much to be desired. They are stopgap measures at best; deadly stultifiers of mental and emotional growth at worst. For more challenging and sustained fulfillment, these are the "games" women play to break free of "The Bored Housewife Syndrome." Following are nine of the most popular categories. Let's examine each, and see what it has to offer:

The Career Game

Perhaps the most popular of all. You've been a housewife for years so now you decide to enter the world of business, which you expect to be stimulating, challenging, exciting. But, after all these years of marriage, how do you do it?

You must first face these facts. You lack specific training, no matter how much education you may have. Unless you have professional training, as a nurse, a teacher, or a hairdresser, for example, you'll need training (or re-training) in a field, either one in which you've already worked or one you'd like to try.

You can't hide behind the old apron and curlers anymore. Take a night school business course; get your typing and shorthand speeds back, if that's your line. Go out and get that training, but no matter what, make sure it's a marketable field.

With skills, sharpened or newly acquired, you're ready for your first interview. Be prepared for the pre-interview jitters. And don't expect the first job you interview for to be offered to you. What will the interview entail? Anything they decide to throw at you, from a simple typing test, to a four-hour, in-depth aptitude exam. You may be soaked with perspiration by the time it's over. You may regret ever having gone. But don't give up the ship!

The first job I ever applied for was with a big insurance company. After extensive testing, I was told I only qualified to sell candy at the lobby concession stand. So much for *my* first try! Go home. Have a good cry. *But don't give up!*

Sometimes it's a good idea to try a smaller company. You may get a chance at a more personal interview. That's how I won my first job. It was a breeze. Within a year I had worked my way up from Front Desk Clerk/Girl Friday to Manager of a forty-unit Motor Inn. It became a rewarding job, and I had a title and a position of responsibility. And what's more, my life now consisted of *giving* orders, wheeling and dealing, meeting and working with entrepreneurs, leaders. Every day was different.

Sounds marvelous, doesn't it. But there are drawbacks. As a result of my achievements, in fact, my husband felt threatened. I could hold my own in the business world—*his* world! This new sense of your own worth *can* create new problems. And as a result, you may wind up suffering as much as before.

Office relationships can become an annoying problem, too—and *I'm* talking about *women!* In a company in which you are one of many female employees, you may be ostracized if you don't conform to the prevalent mode of behavior and dress. *They* eat lunch every day in the company cafeteria, but *you* enjoy getting away for lunch in a restaurant—because you dare to deviate from the established pattern you are an outcast. They fear your independence because it threatens the security they find in conformity.

You don't think about fringe benefits when you're safe and snug at home on a cold, snowy day, and don't *have* to go out if you don't choose to. The up-at-6:30 AM bit, the mad scramble to get everyone fed, dressed and off to school and work on time, the lick and a promise you give the house before you, yourself, get ready to leave for work. Come hell or high water you've got to leave by 7:45. Then it's the out-in-the-cold-weather-to-the-stalled-car-nerve-shattering-traffic-jam routine. At the office, you can't just sit around looking glamorous all day; you've got to *produce*.

As five o'clock rolls around and the business day draws to a close, you drag yourself home. Then there's a family dinner to prepare, a hodgepodge of the day's dishes waiting, an untidy house to straighten, plus piled-up laundry and ironing to do. Believe me, the Career Game is not all fun and frolic!

But back to the plus side of the balance sheet. A paycheck each week, and the knowledge that you are capable of supporting yourself. These are great ego builders. Being able to afford a quiet lunch in an elegant restaurant, visiting the beauty salon once a week for the full treatment, saving for that trip to Europe you've always dreamed of taking, are direct results of a paying job. With a full-time job, in addition to home duties, you won't have time to even *think* about being bored.

The Back-to-College Game

Perhaps you've wanted to find the "lost you" by going back to school. Well you can . . . and prepare for a good job at the same time! You may find killing two birds with one stone quite rewarding.

I recently enrolled in a college summer session. I took "Creative Writing," and "Business Management," and I even managed to pull an "A" and a "B". But more important, attending college again, I discovered an incredibly fascinating world of ideas, of *thinking*. I was "me" again. And I was standing on my own merit. Actually, I was neither working towards a degree nor preparing for a particular job; I was only filling an empty summer.

Even if *you* decide to try the Back-To-College Game, you must remember that few jobs in this day and age, for men *or* women, are 100% creative. Many are so specialized that imaginative thinking is frowned upon.

This Game is better by far than sitting at home. But don't kid yourself: nowadays college degrees are not that rare. At best, a degree can *open a door* to a creative or challenging position, but then it's up to you and your imagination, determination and innate ability.

I have many acquaintances who think they are the greatest, to be fervently applauded and admired just because they are filling the hole in their education by going back to school for some kind of degree. They don't have the faintest idea of how any of these impressive-sounding degrees will help them, but because it's some kind of a status symbol, they line up.

One of my dearest friends is currently in the process of obtaining a Ph.D. in, of all subjects, *philosophy!* Now I ask you: What jobs can she get once that sought-after title of Doctor is earned? Unless you're in it for knowledge for its own sake, or pure status, and simply don't care about (or need) a job, you should consider carefully if your studies will *help* you.

When a woman who's successfully played Back-To-College seeks suitable employment, she may soon discover that employers aren't always that impressed by a degree . . . they want to know what she can *do*.

Although this game is definitely a form of escape from "The Bored Housewife Syndrome," it can be a waste of time and money, unless you are realistic and choose your field of educational endeavor very carefully.

The Club Game

Women of all ages seek escape from boredom by becoming actively involved in women's clubs, whether

31

social or service organizations, many of which make invaluable contributions to the community in many areas.

Some women, however, become compulsive joiners. Some go completely overboard, neglecting their families as a result. Many husbands eat cold beans for supper because their wives spent hours preparing a fancy dessert for a club meeting.

I followed this course once but soon discovered that many women's clubs are superficial, and worse: a waste of time. The club types all seem to possess a strong "herd" instinct. They *need* to belong. Social acceptance is their prime motivation. They *have* to make it somewhere, establish some kind of identity. For them, clubs fill a need. But while they politely sip tea or coffee and munch cookies, many of these women systematically and maliciously tear to pieces absent members of the club. It becomes a way, in their confused minds, to maintain a sense of self-esteem.

Because these women feel threatened by ideas and behavior that contrast with their own, they band together. Pull the strings and these puppets say (and do) all that has been deemed socially acceptable—by the group.

The leaders of women's clubs often satisfy their secret ambition to dominate by leading ("bossing" might describe it!) the "herd." Any woman who has the creativity to suggest innovations or who dares question executive decisions will soon find herself isolated. After a few weeks, she will get the point and resign. (Or at least that's been my experience!) "Don't make waves" is a prime requisite for club joining. If that's your cup of tea, fine. I prefer to brew my own. I can't accept this kind of mindless pressure to conform.

While we're on the subject, I'd like to say a few well-chosen words about nationally chartered social clubs catering exclusively to married couples. I'm not referring to sex clubs ("Key Clubs"). Again, I can only speak from personal experience.

Let me tell you about a typical club function which I attended with my husband—a Valentine's Day party. Arriving at the home of one of the club's officers, we were led to a fantastic "rec room" where the liquor flowed like water. The dancing began almost immediately. Several people asked *us* to dance (it's common practice at these parties for a woman to ask a man to dance with her and it's considered "corny" for a husband to dance with his own wife). As the evening progressed, the open flirting and subtle sexual by-play increased, especially amongst the dancers. The whole thing reminded me of a teen party. Everyone flirting and teasing, but no one *really* doing anything. Frustrated wives use these clubs as a means of alleviating pent-up hatred for men, behaving like what the younger generation call "cock teasers."

These pseudo-seductresses flirt, kiss or pet any available husband, no matter how much this hurts their own husbands or the other men's wives. To satisfy her own ego, this type of woman must prove that she is irresistible to *all* men. By leading a man on, by turning him on and then refusing to follow through, she achieves a feeling of superiority. The sad thing is that this type of woman is frequently frigid. Hating men, she naturally blames her frigidity on them. . . . "It's his fault! I am a vital, sexual woman. *He* failed me."

Women who join couples' clubs merely to build their own egos through flirting, are copping out. They should try adultery. At least it offers them the chance to experience a true relationship.

Another popular solution to "The Bored Housewife Syndrome," the Arts and Crafts Game is more productive than many of the games. This outlet holds boredom at bay, and the women who take this route keep busy from morning 'til night happily working on do-it-yourself projects: sewing their own clothes, drapery making, needlepoint, crewel embroidery, knitting, weaving, candlemaking, *découpage,* glass bottle cutting, tissue paper art, macramé, antiquing, tie-dying, crocheting, etc. Their list of accomplishments is endless; there is almost nothing in the field of home crafts that they can't do. They simply buy themselves a "How-to" book and go to it. The things they create are often truly beautiful and are admired and envied by all.

The arts and crafts player has learned to make constructive use of her time and, by creating, she acquires a justified sense of pride in her accomplishments, not to mention the "see-what-I-can-do" aspect involved. The only real drawback to this game is that it usually excludes personal contact with others. Life goes on around her but she is not *part* of it; she has dropped out and isolated herself within her own home. The Arts and Crafts Game is like masturbation—it's only played alone. How much better it would be if these women got involved in the outside world by taking a night school course in a more demanding craft they wanted to learn: sculpting, pottery, metalwork, etc. At least this would expose them to life and other people, if only for a few hours a week.

A few other outlets in this same vein include organic gardening, raising pets, growing numerous varieties of African violets or other house plants, etc. Some women *do* fill their days with these activities and they *are* creative in their own way.

This game is played with your husband. The goal is togetherness: keep the marriage together by growing and diversifying together. This is a very healthy and workable outlet that is a big step towards keeping a marriage intact, especially one that has gone stale. New interests, new activities and new challenges can make you and your husband see each other as you once were, before the bills, before the mortgage, the children, illnesses, petty grievances, the routine that comprises living together. Instead of finding individual outlets, each in your own separate way, in this game you "try it together."

In this case, playing obviously requires mutual co-operation. This means the husband must tear himself away from the television and the wife must tear herself away from the children or being "Mrs. Clean." If either partner refuses to cooperate, the game won't even get off the ground. But, I have seen many instances where, played properly, it seemed exceedingly beneficial to the couple. I know . . . it's pretty difficult to plan "together" activities with young children and a limited budget. However, the sum delegated to "Entertainment" can mean saving a marriage.

There are many interests that don't cost a fortune. Dance lessons, square dancing, painting, sculpture, drama workshops, book discussion groups, singing or orchestral groups, often involve no fee or only a nominal one. Tennis, golf, swimming, skiing, yoga, bowling, sailing, etc., are for the athletically inclined. There are symphonies, plays, movies, summer stock productions, toastmasters' clubs, lecture groups, gourmet cooking groups. The list is endless.

What does this game accomplish? First (and foremost), it'll help you see each other as individuals again, not a paycheck and a maid. Second, it gives you something to look forward to besides television, an alternative to feeling trapped and bored. Expecting one person to answer to another's needs for variety and stimulation in a marriage without some help can be a crippling demand. This game can be that "helper," and it can alleviate the day-to-day monotony of living together.

Men might possibly find it difficult to give time to outside activities, as their job pressures often tire them out. But once tried, most men find this game a tension reliever, to say nothing of the pleasure of not hearing their wives harp about what a tiring day they've had. This is especially important to the "tied-in-housewife" with small children. The career woman is usually as tired as her husband, but she, too, needs a break from the pressures of her job.

Some couples who are simply not the let's-go-out-and-join-the-crowd type work together on their homes, boats, cars, vacation homes, do-it-yourself projects that run the gamut from painting a house, adding a recreation room, renovating a kitchen, adding a bath, to small projects like building shelves, antiquing furniture that they bought together at auctions or flea markets. This outlet can lead to significant financial savings. You can decorate a house for practically nothing, with the special fringe benefit that each item has special meaning for you, and is a source of lasting pleasure.

The "togetherness couple" doesn't actually look alike, yet in their presence one feels they are indistinguishable. For instance, one begins a sentence and the other one finishes it. They have merged their separate personalities into one. When either stands alone he or she can be at a loss without the missing half. They are merged "for better, for worse, for richer, for poorer

. . . till death do they part" as they pledged in their wedding vows. They are doing it with less monotony, boredom, stress. They are living together, not just existing together.

DESTRUCTION GAMES

The Alcohol Trap

One of the most dangerous reactions to "The Bored Housewife Syndrome" can be the use of alcohol. I'm not talking about social drinking, which, of course, we all do, or even an occasional case of over-indulgence that leads to out-and-out reeling drunkenness. Almost everyone succumbs to that need to escape at some time or other. But the habitual use of alcohol as a means of escape is something else entirely. Something to be avoided at all costs!

Who among us hasn't suffered from a rainy day, when we're trapped indoors with children who are bored and irritable because they can't go out to play, the TV set is on the blink, you're trying to cook, set the table, wash the left-over lunch dishes and referee the children's arguments? All at the same time! You're climbing the walls, so you fix yourself a good, stiff drink before dinner to soothe your frazzled nerves.

It does the job, so you start to make it an afternoon ritual. When "Sesame Street" comes on, the bottle comes out. One afternoon, you find it takes two or three drinks to "relax." Soon, you are reaching for the bottle even *earlier* in the day. Before long, you are having a shot with your second cup of coffee in the morning. (After your husband leaves for work, of course!)

By now, he's mentioned, just in passing, how fast his booze is disappearing. So you juggle the grocery budget in order to buy your *own* private bottle, to hide in a convenient place so you can get to it when you're up-tight and need a drink to see you through. Take my word for it! Secret drinking is a downhill trip, all the way! It'll end up destroying not only your marriage— but probably *you* as well.

The Drug Scene

A big problem, not much discussed until recently, is the habitual use of prescribed drugs (sleeping pills, tranquilizers, anti-depressants, pep pills, diet pills, etc.), by young housewives.

Like problem drinking, a dependence on drugs starts innocently enough. You need help for nerves, you lack energy, have insomnia, or are over-weight, etc. The drugs are prescribed by a doctor in good faith to help his patient. But then she often develops a tolerance and needs a larger and larger dosage to achieve the needed effect. She starts seeing doctor after doctor as a "new" patient to keep up with her ever-increasing demand. Eventually she exhausts her list of doctors and now tries nearby cities, even using fake names and addresses.

When she runs out of doctors her only recourse is the pusher on the street: dexedrine, barbiturates, LSD, pot, heroin—whether dependence is physical or emotional, it's real . . . and really sick!

Women, even kids, can easily buy over-the-counter pills for every physical and emotional disorder. There are no restrictions as to quantity for these legitimate medications, either. Young and old are "popping" these pills to get up, to calm down, to sleep, or for pain, and in combination and quantities at an alarming rate. Although over-the-counter drugs are clearly labeled with warnings about usage, these are widely disregarded.

Indiscriminate drug use combined with alcohol or other drugs can be just like playing "Russian Roulette." Even if the drugs are perfectly legal.

Medications can and do alleviate emotional and physical disorders, or at least their symptoms. But no drug is without some side effect, and when psychological, if not physical, dependency develops, and a drug is used in ever-increasing amounts, those small side effects can be magnified to the point where the "cure" is more debilitating than the problem it was meant to alleviate.

There also appears to be great laxity on the part of many doctors in informing their patient about the drug they have prescribed, its side effects, how it reacts with other drugs, with alcohol, etc. I have personally experienced this situation with several doctors. The patient is not warned as she should be. This is the doctor's *duty,* yet he is often negligent or simply "too busy."

When you get the prescription, how is it labeled? That depends upon state regulations and the doctor's orders. Most give prescription number, the doctor's name, the patient's name, possibly the drug name, the date prescribed, and the name of the pharmacy. Usually that's it, along with directions on dosage, of course. How many prescription bottles carry any warnings? It is indeed possible for a housewife to get "hooked" without knowing what is occurring. Not all patients are under constant supervision. Even if they were, how would it help as long as the doctors aren't more careful about the medication they prescribe? Thousands of people every year die from a fatal combination of drugs and alcohol.

40

Women frequently fall into this trap after a few years of marriage and a child or two. It starts gradually, first one pound, then another. They tell themselves it makes no difference: "I'm not exactly a teenager anymore and it's normal at my age to acquire a more matronly appearance." Then a ten-pound excess becomes twenty more, before they realize what's happening.

Imagine yourself a twenty-nine-year-old, 5 feet 5, weighing 160 pounds. That's what happened to *me!*

Because of my fast-growing family, I found myself spending hours in the kitchen, and you know what that means. A taste here, a sample there. My husband's job kept him out of town a lot and I made up for my loneliness by eating and eating. I looked like a small blimp!

Thanks to my family doctor, I joined Weight Watchers, and slowly I shed the excess pounds . . . and without pills.

It can be done. All it takes is will power. And hard work. That's the *only* way because if you lose weight with diet pills you'll probably regain it once you stop the pills. The *Merck Manual* (the doctors' handbook) says: ". . . nervous tension, frustrations and dissatisfactions may be expressed in increased food intake. . . . Pleasure in eating may become a dominant personality trait and may serve as a substitute when social, business or sexual desires are unsatisfied. Obesity itself may be used as a weapon against undesired contacts or activities, and to justify withdrawal from normal pursuits due to loss of physical attractiveness and efficiency."

How many women do *you* know whom you consider plump or even downright fat? Many unhappy women console themselves by overeating. Some women punish their husbands by becoming fat. (Punish! Who wants to make love to a fatty?) A woman who resents her husband because his job or his hobbies take up so much of his attention will often use food as a consolation for herself—and a turn-off for him. What she may not realize is that in doing this she may well be setting the stage for him to play "The Game."

Overweight can cause serious health problems, too. Obesity predisposes you to heart trouble, hypertension, diabetes and circulatory difficulty (especially in your feet and legs), to mention just a few. So smarten up and slim down! You'll be happier for it. Take my word for it, overeating is a downhill trip.

The Baby Game

"There was an old woman who lived in a shoe; she had so many children that she didn't know what to do —without them."

This probably is the most common form of escape for women.

A woman who plays this game is just like a breeding cow. She has an excessive need to be needed, and who is more dependent than a child? What power a prolific mother possesses: literally surrounded by innocent, adoring, dependent children, with herself in complete control! Her children become her reason for being. Every time the "baby" reaches school age she gets pregnant. In order to keep conceiving, some women will even stop using birth control without their husbands' knowledge or approval. These women are lost without a baby or young child to care for. For them, it's a way to avoid facing the world outside.

Some desperate women will deliberately become pregnant in the hope of holding a straying husband, especially if he happens to have a strong paternal nature. Men realize that 99% of the time when a divorce occurs, the mother gets custody of the children. If he's lucky, the father gets to see them for a few hours a week, thus missing out on the joys of watching their day-to-day growth. Some fathers stay married because of the children.

The truth is that some women capitalize on their children from the day they are born. A child gives them a socially acceptable excuse with which to withdraw from the outside world.

"I'm sorry but I can't attend the town Board of Directors meeting (or the PTA meeting, or my husband's Christmas office party, etc.) because I don't want to leave the baby (who is eight years old) with a babysitter" is a classic example of how this woman will use her children as a rationale for her own reluctance to participate in the world around her. She feels that her main purpose in life, her full-time job, to the exclusion of everything else, including even her husband, is being a mother. Her husband is a meal ticket and an impregnator, and that's about it!

Madonna's children are always on display. Always spotless, dressed in the newest and best while Mother wears the same old suits and dresses she's worn for years. You can spot the type in a minute by the "sensible" shoes they always wear!

This professional martyr presents a false image to the world because in actuality she maneuvers her children to protect herself from herself: she is hiding from the real world. This cookies-and-milk existence is a cop-out and can be harmful to the children if they are over-protected—and they usually are. Mother makes every decision for them, from choosing their friends to picking their wardrobes, even when the "children" are teenagers!

Many women play this game until the day they die.

When their children marry they play Mother-in-law and Grandma, and the mothering continues. Only now it's called interfering. The umbilical cord is never severed!

4

THE ADULTERY GAME

Speaking as a tried-and-true player, I have found that the secret life I now lead is stimulating, educational, fulfilling, challenging, and fun! Adultery can reinforce a marriage that has become boring or routine by making up for what is lacking at home. Playing "The Game" can remedy intellectual boredom, provide fulfilling sex, add glamour to a mundane home existence, and help you live with normal personality clashes. (What if you're an extrovert married to a guy who is gloomy and pessimistic? A Playmate who is basically an "up" person will offset the negative guy you're married to.)

Bear in mind that adultery is a game, an alternative to divorce.

How did *I* first get involved in playing "The Game"? What finally drove me to it? Believe me, even minutes before it actually happened I would have said it was *impossible:* I never dreamed *I'd* be *unfaithful!*

My first affair began unexpectedly. I was a "straight" housewife. I had tried almost everything to escape "The Bored Housewife Syndrome"—everything *except* adultery.

One dreary afternoon, on the spur of the moment, I wrote a fan letter to a local radio-telephone-talk show personality, telling him how much I enjoyed his program that particular day. He was a big celebrity in our area, well-known for his controversial, unique program and famous for his image as a swinger. In fact, women of all ages declared their undying love for him —daily—on-the-air—without fail! He was affectionately referred to as "the housewives' answer to boredom" and my girlfriends and I were great fans of his and sincerely liked his program.

A few days later I received his autographed picture. My girlfriends ate their hearts out with envy! For a laugh, I decided to put him on. Here's the masterpiece of a thank-you letter I wrote:

Dear Paul,

Each afternoon I listen—enraptured—to the sound of your magnificent voice, a faceless voice until yesterday when I received your autographed picture. I realize that I am but one lowly devotee from among your thousands of worshiping listeners, but to me the gift of your picture is priceless.

My life is but an empty shell, a void of nothingness, until you fill it each day. Your every articulate word vibrates with virility. Your every statement is profound. I drink in your vocal presence daily and it nurtures me.

The wonder of you is overwhelming. Since receiving your picture, I have experienced the gratification of seeing the ultimate in physical perfection. There is a flawless union between your mind and body. Mere words are inadequate to describe your exquisite countenance except to say that you are superior to ALL others, in ALL ways. Thank you for being YOU!

Signing the letter, I wondered what—if any—his reaction would be. Secretly I hoped he'd read my letter on-the-air; that would really blow my girlfriends' minds!

Paul's reaction was positive . . . and immediate. The next afternoon, an hour before his show was to go on,

46

the phone rang. It was him, my idol, "the Star!" After chatting for a few minutes, during which time I confessed to being married and a housewife, he hit me with the real purpose of his call: He wanted to know when and where he could meet me for a drink to show his appreciation for my letter! By the time we finished talking, I had somehow been persuaded to meet him *that evening* for a drink! If I had had time to think about it, I never would have gone; I'm sure. I'd have lost my nerve. What would *you* do if, say, Johnny Carson called and invited you to meet him for a drink? Married or not, I *had* to go. Imagine: me meeting a star! This would be a high point of my life!

I wanted to share my good fortune with someone so frantically. I called my best friend, Vicky, a divorcee, who immediately sensed the excitement in my voice and rushed right over. She spent the first hour trying to talk some sense into me, but after realizing how determined I was, and how much meeting Paul meant to me, she pitched in and helped me to get ready for the big adventure.

Frantically we washed and set my hair, plucked my eyebrows and manicured my nails. And then suddenly it dawned on me: I had nothing to wear! My wardrobe consisted of maternity clothes, shirtdresses, and pleated skirts from high school. The only presentable outfit I owned was a five-year-old navy blue and white knit, my "Sunday" dress, which modestly covered my knees! But before my horrified eyes, Vicky changed all that. Snip, snip, and presto: my demure, "Sunday best" was now a stylish mini! Sitting under the hair dryer hemming my new mini, I listened to Paul's program. I had been a fan for years, and although I listened to Paul's program every day without fail, I had never gathered up enough courage to call him on-the-air. The mere sound of his voice sent goose bumps all over my body. His picture only increased my admiration. He was handsome beyond my wildest dreams, tall, well-built, with a distinguished beard, hypnotic eyes, and the most beautiful dimple I'd ever seen! A real turn-on, and tonight I was going to meet him, my dream man, my idol, live and in-person. It was a dream come true. I just couldn't believe it!

As the hour for our meeting approached, I began to lose my nerve. What on earth would we talk about? Where would he take me? What if someone recognized me? What if he didn't like me and was bored stiff? To fortify my faltering courage, I drank my supper: two Screwdrivers! (For me, that's a lot!) If it hadn't been for Vicky, I never would have made it. She fed my children their supper while I took my bath and dressed. My husband was scheduled to work until midnight, so I didn't need an excuse for my absence. I was sure I'd return home before he did, and Vicky was going to babysit.

You just wouldn't believe the transformation that took place at my house that afternoon! The ugly duckling had somehow become a swan! In just four hours a miracle had taken place: my hair was beautifully coiffed, my makeup was just right, and my mini looked breathtaking! I looked stunning.

To calm down, I had another drink—"for the road." As a result, I was both tipsy *and* scared to death when the taxi picked me up. When I arrived at the appointed spot, *he* was waiting! As nonchalantly as possible, I managed to enter his car and mumble "Hello," and our eyes met. My heart actually skipped a beat; in person he was just as I had imagined him. His physical magnetism was beyond belief! We pulled into traffic, heading for an out-of-town bar where we could have a quiet drink without being recognized. Yes, he was also married. He tried—in vain—to make conversation, but I was so overwhelmed by the fact that I was with *him* that I was tongue-tied. I have *never* in my whole life been speechless—until that night!

As we drove along, our conversation went something like this. Anyone over the age of six would have been able to answer his simple questions, but unfortunately, here's what *I* said:

"Well, that was really some letter you wrote. It was really impressive. How did you come up with something like that?"

SILENCE

"Oh . . . I don't know."

"What do you think of my show?"

SILENCE

"I like it."

"Do you listen all the time?"

SILENCE

"Yes."

"But your voice doesn't sound familiar. Have you ever called me on-the-air?"

SILENCE

"No."

"Well, why not? If you listen every day, and I've been on for two years, why have you never called in?"

SILENCE

"Oh . . . I don't know."

PAUSE

"How many children do you have?"

Etc.

Suddenly I realized that the conversation he had initiated about my great letter and his show had fallen flat on its face because of my lack of response, and now he was asking about my children and the old nitty-gritty. My heart sank! I had struck out! Expecting to meet an interesting, sophisticated woman he could intelligently converse with, he now had me pegged, despite my glamourous appearance, as a run-of-the-mill housewife.

Desperately, I tried to think of something to say, but my mind was a blank. Suddenly he pulled the car off the road and stopped. "Oh no," I thought, "we must have a flat tire, and here we are out in the middle of nowhere! How will I ever get home?" And when Paul turned to me, a terrible thought crossed my mind. What if he was some kind of pervert, preying on married women who couldn't complain to the police? I tried to recall what my husband had told me about kneeing a guy in the groin to immobilize him. How did I ever get into *this!*

Then Paul spoke: "You are obviously very ill-at-ease being out with me. Would you like me to take you home?" My relief must have been obvious, for he began to laugh softly, and so did I. The next minute, I found myself in his arms being kissed, and enjoying it! Although no words were spoken, ten minutes later we were in a motel room, in each other's arms, completely oblivious to the world around us. Words were no longer necessary. Up to this point I had done everything wrong, but, in bed, we communicated sublimely. The unbelievably strong physical attraction between us was, at it is now, phenomenal.

By the time Paul and I left the motel it was getting late. Neither of us spoke as we headed for a nearby diner for a much-needed cup of coffee. Sitting there in the restaurant across from him, in that bright and all-revealing light, my embarrassment was obvious. To make matters worse, the waitress and several customers recognized Paul, and as a result we found ourselves surrounded by autograph-seekers and people commenting on his show. I was introduced as his "secretary" (a ploy we often used in the months and years ahead); but that night I was convinced that *everybody* knew

50

the true nature of our relationship, and that it wasn't business!

"Any regrets?" Paul asked, as I basked in the afterglow of our lovemaking. I shook my head. My awe of him blocked my normal loquaciousness, and I sat there groping for words, unable to voice my thoughts and feelings. I felt like a complete idiot, again, but each feelings. I felt like a complete idiot again, but each and remembered what had taken place just a short while ago, I found it difficult to believe that the whole evening wasn't all a dream; that I, a meek, mousey, run-of-the-mill housewife was actually sitting here with a radio personality; that I had willingly committed adultery, had loved every minute of it, and now had no regrets at all! It was a scene right out of a soap opera!

Time passed swiftly, yet I was reluctant to face the prospect of returning home. I was convinced that my husband would take one look at me and know all! Paul assured me that this wouldn't happen, provided I followed my normal behavior pattern. So home I went.

"Home, sweet home." Vicky was pacing the floor, waiting on pins and needles to hear about my big date. How could I tell her what had happened! How could I ever tell *anyone,* for that matter! I entered the house starry-eyed, walking on air. Again I found myself at a loss for words.

"Where did he take you?"

"Uh . . . for a drink."

"Where?"

"Uh . . . I don't remember."

"What did you talk about?"

"Nothing much."

"What is he like in person?"

"Uh . . . nice."

I was so unlike my usual self that Vicky was convinced that Paul had turned me on to LSD and that I was still tripping! She was so upset that she insisted she be allowed to call my family doctor! I *had* to level with her and so proceeded to relate—in detail—what had happened.

She didn't even believe me! She couldn't accept the fact that "straight" me had gone to a motel with some guy I had known less than an hour! Finally I convinced her that I was telling the truth, and she left, shaking her head and muttering: "I can't believe it! No way! Not *you!*"

Following Paul's instructions on what to do when I got home, I quickly bathed and slipped into my pajamas, pretending that I was asleep when my husband came home. My husband never even knew that I had been out. Paul called the following day, and blindly I became entrenched in an affair that was to continue for years.

Paul and I broke almost every rule set forth in this book and in the process very nearly ended up destroying both our marriages. Eventually we managed to develop a relationship that both of us can live with, and we still see each other occasionally.

Can you imagine how difficult it was for me to sit silently with my girlfriends while they discussed Paul and his program when here I was, having an *affair* with him! I began to call him on-the-air after we became involved, and, of course, I remained his biggest fan, but for very personal reasons. No one ever suspected the real reason because I had been a fan of his for years, and I still am!

Adultery fills a human need for direct contact, communication on a one-to-one basis. Suddenly I was not a bored housewife anymore. I had something to look forward to besides sorting laundry, waxing floors, and cleaning messes I hadn't made. I had a secret life. I found myself whizzing happily through humdrum chores and still finding time to wash and set my hair, polish my nails, give myself a facial, shave my underarms and legs, and even squeeze in a bubble bath! I'd think to myself, my euphoria will carry me because tonight, with my Playmate, I'm going to be *"me"*—a woman *not* taken for granted; a woman who is considered fascinating, beautiful, intelligent, desirable, interesting and unique by a *male* to whom I am a person, not a fixture!

5

PLAYING AND STAYING:
YOUR BEST OPTION

If you decide to play "The Game," be prepared to become one of the world's great actresses. You'll literally lead a double life, playing an enormous variety of roles, from nun to prostitute. Once you know how, it's a lot easier than you might first imagine.

How often do *you* put your husband on, turning on the tears, for instance, to get your way? Be honest! When I find myself engaged in a senseless argument with my husband and know that continuing the discussion will result in one of us saying the kind of things that are definitely best left unsaid, I frequently resort to tears as a way of ending the whole thing.

How often do *you* smile through tightly-clenched teeth? Make polite, social conversation with someone you *detest?* (Your mother-in-law? Your husband's boss?) *Never?* Whether you realize it or not, you do it all the time. In fact, we all (and I don't mean just housewives, either) do it so automatically that most of the time we don't even realize it. For instance, how often do you say: "Hello, how are you?" to a neighbor or casual acquaintance without actually caring at all? It's a matter of just being polite, right? This is the kind of put-on social scientists call "the language of social cohesion," yet a put-on, nevertheless.

You *can* act a part if you have to. And if you play "The Game" acting is a necessity.

You must be ready to play your role to the hilt, or risk a slip-up and static, static that can take a range of forms from arguments and tension to actual divorce proceedings. Even if you never play "The Game," it would still be helpful to learn at least the first two rules. These two commonsense precepts can help put your marriage on a more even keel:

1. *Earn Your Keep. Give Your Husband His Money's Worth.*

When you choose to play "The Game," you must accept it for what it is—diversion from your primary responsibility, that is as a wife and a mother.

Does your husband support *you?*

All right then, what do *you* do to earn your keep? You know he's entitled to and deserves certain services from you in return for the financial support he provides. He has the right to expect meals on a reasonable schedule, an orderly house, clean clothes, peace and quiet while he reads the evening paper, the privilege of sleeping late on weekends, being able to take a bath without first having to scrub the tub, and most importantly, a willing sex partner. Never mind the "I'm too tired tonight" routine. Remember, if all he wanted was an immaculate house, hot meals and laundry service, he could hire a housekeeper. Have intercourse whenever he wants. Fake enthusiasm if necessary but do it when he wants to do it. (See the section on "How to Develop Your Potential.")

If you shut him off sexually, or act like you're only submitting to his animal desires, you will pay with sweat and tears. You will have an irritable, sarcastic husband, a tense household. A turned-down, turned-off husband is a husband who just might decide to play "The Game" himself. What he can't get at home, he'll

55

probably look for elsewhere, and that's a fact! Who knows, he might even divorce you. If that's your goal, fine. If you think you can take on the cold, cruel world alone, go ahead, cop out as a wife. To stay or not to stay? It's your decision.

But if you do stay then you must play the role—wife, homemaker and lover—to the best of your ability. Give it all you've got. Think of your marriage as a Broadway play where mediocre performances are not tolerated, and a stand-in lurks just around the corner. Your hamburger may be somebody else's steak. Keep that in mind. As long as you are the perfect wife, your husband will never suspect you're playing "The Game."

2. *Stop Complaining*.

Assuming you've been married awhile, the guy isn't exactly a stranger. By now you know him like a book. So just what do you expect to accomplish by constantly nagging him about picking up his dirty socks or straightening up his closet? Calling him a lazy slob doesn't accomplish much, either—except alienating him. You've been picking up after him for years; stop complaining. You're not going to change him at this late date.

My own dear, sweet husband used to *drive me up a wall* because he steadfastly and adamantly refused to wear pajamas. He prefers to sleep in his underwear. Did I nag or pitch-a-bitch? You bet! But to no avail naturally. I have since learned to accept what I can't change. I've stopped constantly trying to make him conform to the mold I think he should fit. As a result, our home is much more peaceful. Constant arguing about unimportant matters is a waste of time and energy. Why scream like a shrew because he left the cap off the toothpaste tube again and it fell down into the sink drain? Smile instead! Why send him off to work filled with memories of you, snarling over some trivial matter? He may decide not to come home!

My husband, for instance, has very definite ideas on just about any subject you mention. Needless to say, he always thinks he's right so it's useless to argue. I simply smile and say, "You're entitled to *your* opinion." Why should I spend an entire evening trying to refute his statement that my hairdresser is a homosexual, when he's absolutely convinced that *all* hairdressers are gay. He's always right, no matter how wrong he may be, so it's a losing battle.

The secret is to let your husband *think* that he's King of the Castle, that your whole world revolves around him. After all, if you are playing "The Game" you're getting what *you* want, aren't you? So play it his way at home and keep him happy. You *gain* more than you lose.

3. *Dress Appropriately For What You're Supposed To Be Doing.*

If you leave the house on the pretext of attending a Cub Scout den mothers' meeting all decked out in the new backless, hot pink cocktail dress you just bought (on sale, of course), he's not going to buy your story.

The trick is to carry an over-sized handbag, containing all you need: a small purse, shoes, panty hose, jewelry, make-up, even a permanent-press dress or pants suit! After all, if your excuse is that you're going to sit in on a "Modern Lit" course at a local college, it's logical to be wearing jeans or slacks, a sweater and sneakers. Dress for the occasion you describe, and change later if necessary. Your transformation can take place in a convenient gas station's Ladies' Room. It takes only a few minutes and it's an important precaution. Dress as plainly and unsexily as possible when your husband is around. Let him think that no man in his right mind would ever give you a second glance. Then you've got him exactly where you want him.

Don't be overly enthusiastic about going to a meeting either. Complain about the bother, or how boring you expect it to be, or the great TV show you're missing for some dull meeting. If possible make him feel sorry for you.

When my night out comes to an end, I shed my glad rags (using the same method I did to don them), jump back into my frumpy old outfit, and into the house I go.

Cool it at home. Never change normal behavior patterns. If you're playing with a stimulating Playmate, you'll probably feel as if you're walking on air much of the time. But if you act this way, at home, your husband is either going to think you've flipped your lid, become an acidhead, *or* you have something going!

Say you usually wake up grumpy, and generally unfit to live with until you've had a cup of coffee. Now what do you think he will think if, all of a sudden, you're up at the crack of dawn, humming and smiling to yourself. He'll faint from shock: YOU smiling at 7:00 AM! Then he'll start wondering what the hell's going on. Why is she so happy?

So cool it; suppress your joy. At least until after he leaves for work!

Once, when I was just learning "The Game," I almost gave the whole show away. A compulsive record collector, I play my stereo constantly. Without thinking, I found myself playing the romantic, dreamy albums of a popular male vocalist my Playmate and I used to listen to together. I began playing these twenty-four hours a day, day after day. My husband couldn't understand my sudden concentration on this particular artist because my musical tastes normally varied from day to day. Fortunately, I realized soon enough that what I was doing could give me away.

Another important precaution: always keep in touch with your "straight" girlfriends. If you are in the habit of dropping in at Linda's at least once a week for coffee, don't stop! If you withdraw from your friends, they'll wonder what's wrong. Are you angry? Offended? They'd never understand if you told them about your secret life, so don't tell them anything. Remembering to keep up these contacts will be hard at first. When you play "The Game," you are naturally inclined to keep to yourself more because you will have so much more to think about and do, like reading a new book your Playmate recommended, or a book on his favorite sport. And sitting with a "straight" woman, no matter how fond you are of her and how close you are, you'll sometimes feel you're living in a soap opera.

4. Never Admit Anything!

Suppose you're burning the proverbial candle at both ends, staying out late several nights a week and in general ignoring and/or discarding the rules I've been spelling out for you. If your husband gets suspicious (and I guarantee he will if you don't stick to the rules) you must lie as if your life depended on it. As indeed it may! To allay suspicions, you must cool it for a time. Stay home for several weeks straight. Only go out for the most legitimate of reasons—and have him pick you up afterwards. Get him to take you out to dinner, perhaps with another couple, and let him see for himself how time can slip by when you're talking and enjoying yourselves. You, of course, will do everything in your power to keep the conversation lively and centered on him!

Play the role of subservient wife to the hilt. Cook his favorite meals. Plan a quiet dinner for two by candlelight. Buy a sexy nightgown and seduce *him* for a change. Do anything and everything possible to erase his suspicions, but *never* admit anything! Confession may be good for the soul, but for a marriage, it can be disastrous.

6

YOUR EXIT: HOW AND WHEN
TO MAKE IT

There are millions of plausible excuses to "exit left" for a few hours (or so) in the evening.

One year I volunteered to work on a PTA talent show. Rehearsals were held once a week for four months. Oh, the beauty of it! I'd leave the house around 7:00 PM, go to rehearsals for an hour or two, then slip away to do my thing. I'd return home about midnight, and if questioned as to what took so long, I'd say I had gone over to so-and-so's house (naming some woman in the show that my husband didn't know) and that my being delayed was due to a late work session. I am certainly no great talent but because the show needed acts so desperately I threw together a brief comedy skit, and this actually did necessitate several extra hours of rehearsing—which I accomplished during the day with the other two "straight" gals who performed the skit with me. We had a marvelous time sewing our own costumes and practicing, and I had an excuse to get out at night!

Another ruse I've used is the bowling league ploy. I joined a women's bowling team as an alternate, and on those nights that the team didn't require my services, I went elsewhere. If I did have to bowl, I'd take off after I was finished. This one got me out once-a-week for one whole summer.

Going to a movie with a gal who is also playing "The Game," and needs an excuse herself, is another possibility. If you use this one, be sure to read a review of the movie you are supposedly going out to see so that you can fake it, if necessary.

Enrolling for various night school courses (adult education at the local high school or community college, etc.) is another perfect "out." And who's to know if you occasionally cut a class because of more interesting activities. Unless, of course, one of your "straight" neighbors is also enrolled. In this case, be extra careful. Develop a sudden headache just after the class begins, show signs of being in pain, and tactfully leave.

Once in a while, you can pretend you are going to a meeting of some kind. If you must really attend one, you can still go out after the meeting is over.

Use your imagination. If you want to play, you'll find excuses to satisfy even the most suspicious husband.

If you sense that your husband is beginning to wonder about the real reason behind your evenings out, try meeting your Playmate during the day. He can pretend he has a business lunch. (Naturally, you're the "business.") Make sure you're home in plenty of time to have dinner on the table. And don't forget to remove all traces of make-up and to jump into an "at-home" outfit.

Here's another great cover: the 5—9:30 PM shopping excuse. Get together with your Playmate after work. Since most stores in large suburban shopping centers are open until 9:00 or 10:00 PM at least two days a week, this gives you four hours of play. Remember, it's primarily the lateness of the hour that makes husbands suspicious. Whatever you do, be sure to arrive home with some purchases, even if only a dress pattern and a spool of thread! Better yet, pick up something for him, a new shirt, a few handkerchiefs. Then how can he complain?

Career Girl Excuses

If you're a career girl, one problem is solved—you're normally attractively dressed, coiffed and made-up.

But what are the appropriate excuses for not heading for home at five every night? It depends, to a degree, on your occupation.

If you work in an office, call and say that there's a rush job, that you must get it out tonight and that it was just handed to you 10 minutes ago! "What can I do?" you say, all perplexed. If he trusts you or has job pressures himself, he will understand unless you pull the same excuse two or three times a week!

Or you could try the old "my-car-won't-start" excuse: "Dear, I'll be home as soon as I can get it going. One of the girls is taking me over to a garage now. I'll see you as soon as I can . . . no, I'll ring you later. Okay?" But don't use this one too often (unless your car is fifteen years old and really falling apart.)

Sometimes a small office party lasts hours more than expected. In which case you could always call home and say, "Dear, you know that girl in our department I told you was leaving? Well, the girls are giving her a farewell party so I might be an hour or two late." It's not a lot of time, I admit, but it's good for a starter.

As a secretary, for instance, sometimes you are asked to run errands for the boss, such as picking up a birthday gift for the boss's wife or daughter. You, of course, take care of it on your lunch hour and then call your husband and tell him you've been asked to

63

pick out a gift for the boss's wife and it must be done immediately.

"The nerve of that guy," fumes your husband.

"But dear," you reply, "I can't refuse—it's my job! You understand, don't you? I'll be home as soon as I can."

Occasional Excuses

A friend is in trouble and you have to stay with her.

You tripped and fell and have to go to the hospital emergency room to have your elbow examined. (Then go and buy yourself an Ace bandage.)

Your brakes gave out and have to be fixed immediately.

Your windshield wipers are shot and it's pouring rain.

A bad traffic jam.

You missed the bus.

Stuck at the beauty parlor.

A career meeting or seminar.

You're going to visit a friend in the hospital.

The husband (or wife) of someone at the office died and you have to pay your respects.

Your car is in a parking lot and you can't find the attendant or you've parked on the top level of a garage and the lift isn't working.

A Word of Caution

Limit your nights out to not more than one a week. One every two weeks is better still. The name of the game is discretion. Remember, too much of a good thing can be dangerous. The fastest way to make your husband suspicious is to suddenly with no plausible explanation, start going out several nights a week.

Your husband isn't going to appreciate some flimsy pretext for your leaving him alone to fend for himself. If the situation were reversed and suddenly he began working late three or four nights a week, what would you think? Especially if he had never worked overtime in all the years you'd been married.

It's difficult for a woman to slip away for a fun-filled weekend with her Playmate. Don't try it unless you have an air-tight alibi. The risk can be greater than the rewards.

Warning!

I have learned from experience that on the nights I go out my husband usually wants to make wild and passionate love when I return. In his case, absence does make the heart grow fonder!

Be prepared and willing to play "sex symbol" (otherwise known as "responsive wife"). Give him what he wants. You should fake enthusiasm, even if you made love with your Playmate less than an hour ago. This is a crucial test and may just require your greatest performance ever.

You may be lucky and find him fast asleep, in which case you can slip quietly into bed.

But for heaven's sake, never wake him! Let sleeping husbands lie. That's what I always say.

7

HOW *NOT* TO FIND
A PLAYMATE

Okay, you've decided to play "The Game." But that doesn't mean that every man you know or come into contact with is a possible Playmate! Get that idea out of your head—immediately! In fact, most of the men you now know are unconditionally *off limits*.

If you are "just" a housewife, most of the men you know are your husband's friends and business associates, relatives, in-laws, and friends' husbands. Right? I'm sorry, but *all* of these men are *out*. I can hear you moaning, but believe me, these men are just too close to home to become involved with sexually. The risk is too great.

With the following men, restraint is strongly indicated:

Your Husband's Friends and Business Associates

What a husband doesn't know won't hurt him, *but* if you get involved with one of his pals, one of the men he works with, his boss or any man with whom he does business, you are putting your husband, yourself, and your Playmate in a precarious position.

If you pick a Playmate who already knows your husband, and has frequent contact with him, it stands to reason that sooner or later his relationship with your husband will suffer. Your Playmate will feel self-conscious, ill-at-ease and guilty every time he looks at your husband. If he's a fishing, golfing, or card-playing buddy, he will begin to make excuses for why he can't go out for the usual eighteen holes or Saturday fishing trip, etc. If they're friends, their friendship will suffer, and if it's his boss you become involved with, he may end up getting fired.

Your Playmate might even feel so guilty about the whole thing that he'll decide to fix matters by telling all to your husband, and then begging forgiveness (especially if the affair has cooled off!). Where would that leave *you?* As likely as not in a divorce court!

Injured pride is probably one of the major causes of divorce. It's a big blow to a husband's ego to find out his wife is "cheating"—but it's a lot worse if he discovers that his wife's lover is one of his friends.

If you discovered that your husband had been unfaithful—and with one of your friends—how would you feel? Wouldn't it be easier to forgive and forget if he'd slept with someone you didn't know?

Laura, a close friend of mine, became involved with one of her husband's co-workers. They had met quite innocently at the office Christmas party. In fact, her husband was the one who introduced them. They danced together a couple of times, talked briefly, and that was that, or so it *seemed.* But two days later when Roy called, she had just had an argument that morning with George (her husband), and was fuming over it. Her afternoon was free, so she agreed to meet Roy for lunch.

One thing led to another and eventually they had an affair. Soon her husband was commenting on Roy's "sudden change in attitude." As design engineers, they often worked together closely on assigned projects. But now Roy seemed to be acting strange. Now he preferred "working alone," and even turned down several luncheon invitations, although they usually lunched together three or four times a week. Poor George didn't know what the problem was. But Laura did!

She had enough sense to end it. But the damage was already done. Her husband's relationship with Roy was never the same again, and before long her Playmate requested a transfer to another department. It could have turned out a lot worse.

Your Girlfriends' Husbands

This type of entanglement puts *you* behind the eight ball. What if you've spent the previous evening painting the town red with your girlfriend's husband, and the following morning *she* drops in for coffee. You're supposedly her friend, so she tearfully confesses how upset she is because she suspects her husband is involved with another woman. How are you going to feel? How will you give her sympathy and understanding when "the other woman" is *you?*

Suppose the *four* of you are good friends and enjoy each other's company? You see quite a bit of each other, socially, often getting together to go swimming, picnicking, or out for pizza and beer. Will you be able to talk and act like nothing is happening the next time the four of you go out together? Or will you be ill-at-ease, nervous and tense? Your husband and your girlfriend may both sense that something is amiss.

It stands to reason that one relationship will suffer as a result of the other. It is quite natural and common for people of the opposite sex who like and admire each other and who see each other frequently, to become physically attracted to each other. A close relationship between a man and woman on a purely platonic level is almost impossible. If you sense that your girlfriend's husband is becoming strongly attracted to you, *back off!* The destruction of two families could result. It's just not worth the risk.

Take it from me, I know! I almost made the sad mistake of becoming involved with the husband of a girlfriend, a gal I saw several times a week, a couple my husband and I spent quite a bit of time with and it happened before I realized the big mistake I almost made. (I *didn't* get involved and had no intention of doing so!)

It all started innocently. Lou stopped by occasionally to borrow my husband's power tools, or fishing equipment. He'd always come over when he knew I'd be alone. I became his "crying towel," a sympathetic ear for all his troubles. One evening after an especially hectic day, he stopped by. My husband had gone to a hockey game in another city, the kids were in bed, and Lou's wife was at night school. When he suggested that "we" go out for a drink I assumed his wife would be coming, too. I called a baby sitter and off we went to a local lounge where I thought we would be meeting his wife after her class. How wrong I was!

Seated in a quiet, secluded corner of the lounge, he reached for me. Putting his arms around me, he tried to kiss me! I pulled away but his hands were all over me. He told me that he loved me and that he expected to have sex with me—if not that night, then some night soon! I quietly told him off, excused myself to go to the powder room and then slipped out the back door and headed home.

The phone was ringing when I walked in. It was Lou, of course. He was convinced that I was in love with him but just wouldn't admit it. I hung up. I still wasn't sure what to do, however, as I paced the floor waiting for my husband to return from the hockey game. Finally, I decided to tell my husband exactly what had occurred. Calmly relating what had happened, I, of course, stressed that I had expected Jenny to meet us at the lounge.

My husband and I decided that we had better cool it with this couple, although my friendship with Jenny continued until they moved away a few months later. I wonder if Lou's damaged ego was the motive for their move?

Relatives and In-Laws

The biggest *no* of all. The most destructive and dangerous of involvements.

Don't start getting any ideas about that living doll your sister is married to, even though you know he is as strongly attracted to you as you are to him. Stop and seriously consider the consequences before you get involved. Your sister would never forgive you. And your husband probably wouldn't, either. The other members of the family would be up-in-arms, too.

Remember, the woman always gets the blame. And let's face it, she usually calls the shots. She provokes, she sends out the signals and she doesn't get involved unless she *wants* to! It's the woman who must keep a situation from getting out of hand.

One nasty situation involved a friend and her brother-in-law. Len was married to June's sister, Sandy. Sandy had a ruptured appendix and when serious complications set in, ended up spending almost a month in the hospital. During her stay, June took care of her sister's two-year-old daughter. Since the child wasn't in school yet, she stayed at June's place round the clock.

It was only natural for her father (June's brother-in-law), to drop in daily to visit and play with his daughter. Working nights, Len spent his days between the hospital and June's house. Kindhearted June insisted

70

that he eat with them and even did his laundry! Eventually, Len made a pass at her, right in her own kitchen in broad daylight! Momentarily, she responded to his kisses and caresses. Suddenly, June's husband walked in and *caught them in the middle* of an embrace!

Nothing of consequence had actually happened, but June's world came crashing down around her. Her husband went into a rage and threw Len out of the house, breaking June's jaw in the tussle. He will never believe that his wife's relationship with her brother-in-law had not progressed beyond that kitchen embrace, and will taunt and torment her with that for years. The family ties are badly damaged and, in typical double-standard logic, June is held responsible.

If it could happen to her (and I assure you that June was "straight," and had never played "The Game") it could happen to you.

The Boss and Your Immediate Supervisors

It's not worth the static, and luckily, the majority of men in offices are deathly afraid of asking a female co-worker out. Think of the consequences should she "kiss and tell!" If *you* become involved with someone, who will be the one to quit—you or him? That's what it boils down to, *especially* after the affair is over.

Another problem: your fellow employees will take note of your every look, action and remark, and out of jealousy might decide to call your husband or your Playmate's wife to "discuss" your extended luncheons and conferences with the boss, or those long "behind-closed-doors" meetings, or to point out how often you've been working over-time together.

Take my own boss fiasco:

I was a Girl Friday for a development corporation. It was a one-girl office and I was instrumental in setting up, furnishing and organizing this new branch office. For once, I loved my job. It challenged me to the fullest. I had been promised a full-time career with profit-sharing, possibly even a partnership! Within three weeks, I had set up the office and it looked beautiful. My boss was president of the company: a handsome six-foot-charmer with wide shoulders, black hair and sparkling brown eyes.

We worked alone together day after day. I learned that familiarity does not always breed contempt because, although we fought it, we found we were distracting each other. Eric would lean over to check a paper while I was arranging the files and the physical attraction was evident. A new man was coming in to take over as president, soon—a former bank vice president and Congressional Representative from that district. He had not yet moved in fully and I saw him only occasionally, since I worked part-time.

But, meanwhile, Eric and I were alone together too much. He made no attempt to ask me out, nor did I encourage such meetings. But one morning as I was making his coffee the way he liked it, he came over and stood behind me . . . I don't really know exactly what happened next, but without warning, I was wrapped in this handsome six-footer's arms, and as I pushed him away, I thought "I'm saying no, but my eyes are betraying me!"

We agreed with shamed faces that we wouldn't let it happen again. But, a few days later, after calling me into the Conference Room, Eric steered me into an alcove and we got pretty intimate, that is, as intimate as you can get in an empty hall with the front office door open to the public! This time I said: "Eric, if this happens again, I'll have to quit. Let's hope Tom's moving in will stop this once and for all."

Thomas, the new man, was now coming in more frequently. The problem seemed to be solved. Then, on the day before Christmas, Eric, who hadn't been his usual self for several days, came over to me. "I have bad news," he said. "The owner (whom I had never met) notified me that you've got to go. He's transferring one of the girls down from headquarters to take your place. There will be a general corporate re-organization and this office will manage only existing property. I'm terribly sorry. I'll give you two weeks' severance and a letter of recommendation."

I'd only been with the firm a few weeks. Tears formed in my eyes, streaking my make-up as I packed my belongings, and took one last look at the Christmas decorations I'd so painstakingly put up, and the two identical gifts for my bosses sitting on the table. As Eric handed me my check, I noticed that he looked guilt-stricken. I took the check, shoved the rest of my things into a bag, said goodbye, somehow, and walked out on a career that had seemed to offer the world to me.

What do *you* think? Did sex with my boss ruin my job, or would this have happened regardless? I'd like to believe Eric's explanation—but do you?

Playmate's Friends

If an affair with a Playmate is over and one of his friends, someone your ex-Playmate introduced you to, calls or you unexpectedly meet one of them and he asks for a date, refuse! Why? Most men are possessive and your ex-Playmate's pride will be injured if you hook up with one of his friends. Also, his friend won't have much respect for you. You've just had one affair that he knows of. If you become involved with him, he will classify you as an easy make!

So watch it—and don't give in. Cool it, play it "straight" and say, "Sorry, but I'm just not interested."

And whatever you do, don't discuss your ex-Playmate with his friends or disclose why you stopped seeing each other. A little discretion goes a long way.

Okay, if you're a housewife, with what other men do you come into contact regularly who could be considered a prospective Playmate?

The milkman?

The mailman?

The insurance man?

Your friendly neighborhood pharmacist or grocer?

Forget it, gals! These men are exposed to women all day, day after day, week in, week out. I have a friend who's a mailman. His day wouldn't be complete without at least one proposition. Some women routinely greet him at the door, naked, or almost naked. They get their mail, but a male is what they're after! As for insurance men, their jobs are on the line every time they make a house call to collect a monthly premium or sell a new policy. One false move, one complaint from a female customer, and they find themselves unemployed!

Don't waste yourself on these guys. It's hopeless.

8

FINDING A PLAYMATE

Now, let's move on to a more agreeable topic, namely how and where to find a suitable Playmate. If you're a career girl, you're out in the world among eligible men five days a week. You meet and have to deal with (besides the to-be-avoided co-workers), sales representatives from other companies, men from other departments, etc. If you decide to take the plunge, it will probably be after a period of informal association and, hopefully, by this time, you should have some idea of what you're getting into.

If you're a working girl, and there's someone you think you'd like to play with (someone you don't work for, say a guy from another department) who's been giving you the eye for months, the next time you're both alone, casually suggest having lunch together.

Let him know you think eating alone is a drag. Offer to go "Dutch." He'll get the message and if he accepts your innocent offer you know he's interested. If he doesn't—forget it! Don't pursue him, he obviously doesn't want to play. After you've had lunch or a drink after work, and you've had a chance to talk a bit and generally gotten to know each other a little better, you'll be in a better position to assess the possibilities. But don't come on too strong—let nature take its course!

Or take co-educational night courses (as long as your husband doesn't come along), such as "Income Tax Preparation" or "The Stock Market," or any other course that attracts large numbers of men. (Some of the teachers aren't bad, either.)

Do hospital volunteer work. You'll meet plenty of male patients and doctors, too.

Get into politics. Work for the party or candidate of your choice. Political organizations always need people to address flyers, stuff envelopes, etc., and your help will genuinely be appreciated.

Suppose you're a "boxed-in" housewife and can only slip away occasionally. How do you meet interesting men? It isn't easy! In fact, one of the few real disadvantages of being a woman is that it is difficult to go Playmate-hunting alone. My best advice is that you seek out a woman who is presently playing "The Game" and knows the whole scene although I must warn you that that's not always so easy, either. At least in the beginning, there is no reliable formula for determining whether a woman is playing "The Game" or not. In fact, that is one of "The Game's" great advantages. But keep looking because whether you believe it or not you do know someone.

One of your best friends may be an active player. Now think carefully, you'd be surprised (maybe even shocked!) at who plays and who doesn't. I lived next door to a woman for over a year without *ever* suspecting that she was playing "The Game."

We spent hours together over coffee, discussing everything, from Nixon's trip to China to toilet training, but it was only by accident that I learned about her secret life. One night my Playmate and I were entering our motel room when all of a sudden I saw this woman, my next-door neighbor, strolling out of the room next to ours in search of an ice machine. We were both speechless! We passed each other without a sign of recognition.

The next morning, after the children had left for school and our husbands for work, my neighbor dropped in and we had a cup of coffee, talked about the night before and swore each other to secrecy. We've been great friends ever since. Now we go out together occasionally looking for new Playmates. (You can't go Playmate-hunting alone!)

I've found that one way to locate other soul-mates who are either playing now or would like to be is by looking for women who somehow stand out. It's nothing specific, but it's something you can sense nevertheless.

A woman who wants to play but doesn't quite know how will often subtly voice her discontent, or she'll admit that she feels that marriage is not the end-all, be-all. Invite her over for coffee and broadly hint around. Then come right out and admit that you'd like to "get away from it all" some night, go out for a drink or two and a few laughs. Usually, if she's playing (or would like to), she'll quickly second the motion. Then you're on your way. As with everything else, the hardest part is getting started. Remember, the first is the worst!

WARNING: Avoid like the plague *any* married woman who plays around and has acquired a reputation. If you let yourself become associated with her you will be given her brand. You know the old saying, "Birds of a feather . . ." Discretion at all costs should be your motto from the moment you begin.

Assuming you now have someone to hunt with, where do you start looking? Obviously, it's safer to play away from home. Here's how: Buy a *Mobil Travel Guide* for your area and pick out several posh, out-of-town restaurants, cocktail lounges or bars that feature dancing. Stay away from clubs with rock bands, if you can, because most men over thirty-five don't know how to dance to this type of music. Pick a place and then go to it! You may strike out your first time out: the place may turn out to be a "complete bomb," no action. So have one drink and leave—the night is still young. Try another spot. Sooner or later you'll hit pay dirt.

Most large, well-known hotels and motels are over-run with men. And the beauty of it is that these hotels and most of these motels have lounges in which their guests may wile away the hours. I can guarantee that a trip to one of these lounges will result in meeting a man. But unless business brings him to town often, the chances are good that you won't see him again.

Warning

Except in a large metropolitan area if you meet someone staying at a hotel, under no circumstances allow yourself to be persuaded to go up to his room for a nightcap. It's not your new acquaintances you have to worry about—it's the desk clerk who's the problem. I mean, face it! What is he supposed to think if he sees a woman going upstairs after midnight with a man she just met? He usually does the "arranging" (if a guest wants a companion), and he will feel you are cutting into his "action." Of course, he assumes that you're a prostitute.

So, if you do make a habit of dropping in at a specific hotel, I'd strongly advise you to confine your activities to the lounge! If some conscientious employee were to tip off the Vice Squad, you could find yourself in a rather unpleasant situation.

Do you feel a little nervous about walking into a

78

strange bar or cocktail lounge? Here's how to play it. Carry some packages and pretend that you and your girlfriend just stopped in for a drink after a hectic shopping spree. Or keep looking anxiously at your watch, the clock on the wall, and the door, pretending that you are waiting for someone. If you're in a group, pretend that you were all on your way home from a meeting and decided, on the spur of the moment, to stop in for a drink.

The men you meet, talk to and dance with in a bar will all inquire, sooner or later, as to your marital status; how you play it is up to you. I usually say that I'm "separated." Later, if the relationship develops I level with him. Most men you meet in bars, cocktail lounges, etc., lie about *their* marital status. They will say that they are divorced, separated, or unhappily married. Don't, under any circumstances, believe a word they say, at least until you know them better. You may be bored with the guy after just a couple of hours of talk and dancing. So what difference does it make if you've lied to him? You may never see him again, anyway. On the other hand, if you've admitted right off that you're married, he'll figure that all you're looking for is a change-of-pace sexually and he will do his level best to convince you that *he* should be it!

Only go to "first class" places. That's where the best men go. Look as innocent as possible; no heavy make-up or low-cut dresses. Go where there's dancing because dancing gives men an excuse to approach you, an opportunity for socially acceptable physical contact.

Never look in second-rate dives or honky-tonk bars. These places are full of losers. You want a worthwhile Playmate. The men in these bars are usually seedy and grabbing, a lot more distasteful than what you've got at home.

Another place to stay away from is the youth hang-out—the kind of place that usually features a rock band. If you look young, fine . . . except the boys you meet in these places are so adolescent, they're more likely to turn you off than on.

Let's assume that you and your girlfriend find a swinging lounge, plenty of handsome men, soft lights, mood music, etc. How do you make the most of this opportunity, so rich in possibilities? First, head for an empty table, preferably in the center of the room. Don't hide in dark corners, and *never* sit at the bar. Okay, now you're sitting demurely, surrounded by a multitude of possible Playmates; you sip your drink diffidently. (Actually, it helps to drink your first drink as fast as you can because you'll probably be nervous, and if someone asks you to dance you may be stiff and uncoordinated. So drink that first one fast, *then* take it nice and slow.)

The band is playing. A "prospect" comes over. Now what? Never dance with an obvious drunk. If one *insists,* or wants to sit down with you, call the waitress. She'll handle it for you. Never dance with a man who completely turns you off on sight. You're wasting your time *and* his. Politely refuse. If he's insistent, be firm.

After dancing with a man once, if you don't like him, don't dance with him again, and don't let him buy you a drink or join you either. Remember, if a guy bothers you, you don't have to sit there and take it. You're a paying customer—you don't owe anyone anything!

The band is playing a cha-cha and a fantastic guy asks you to dance, and you don't know the step. Ask for a rain check. Maybe he'll offer to teach you. Get up and try it, what have you got to lose?

Occasionally, the waitress will arrive with drinks, "compliments of the gentlemen at the bar." Accept the drinks, and smile a bright "thank you." Within five minutes, the guy (usually two guys) will approach your table and want to join you. Let them sit down. Then, if you decide they are not your type, get rid of them with "The Silent Treatment." This means: answer *all* their questions with a yes, no, or shrug. Ignore them completely. They'll get the message.

What if your girlfriend likes one of them and you can't stand his friend? Just sit there and ignore his friend. When the band starts playing and he asks you to dance, refuse. Suggest that he ask someone else. Go to the Ladies Room and pray he's dancing with someone else by the time you get back. If necessary, get sarcastic as hell. If some other guy asks you to dance, accept even if he's worse than the one you're trying to shake.

If a guy starts making suggestive remarks, like "I bet you're great in bed," either while you're dancing or sitting together, ask him to leave the table or walk off the dance floor.

Another *no* is listening to obscene jokes. Men who tell dirty jokes to women do so, at least in part, out of a lack of respect; also to size you up by your reaction. They are primarily looking for someone who is willing to head immediately for the nearest motel. If that's all we wanted, we'd stay at home.

Dancing gives you a good opportunity to get near potential Playmates, but it does have its hazards. Imagine that you're dancing with a marvelous guy for the first time. He's holding you close; the band's playing one of your favorite songs; everything is beautiful. Suddenly you're aware of a hand moving slowly down your back towards your bottom and he's pressing your pelvis against his erect penis, trying to "dry screw" you! If that happens, walk off the dance floor, fast! The guy is saying, in essence, "You look like an easy make." Most likely after you walk off, he will follow you back to your table, apologizing all over the place, explaining that he just couldn't control himself, with you so close.

81

Tell him to get lost! He's an animal! You don't need him!

It's another story if, after dancing with a guy for some time, he gets an erection which you can feel faintly as you dance. It merely means that he finds you attractive. It's *how* he reacts, what he *does* about it, that tells the story. He will probably back off a tactful few inches, but, again, if he pushes and rubs it against you like an adolescent, *walk away!*

Always carry enough money to pay for your own drinks. Hustling drinks is definitely not the name of the game! Pay your own way *unless* he insists on picking up the tab, and has spent the evening with you. But use your judgment.

You may want to see him again, but don't give him your last name or phone number. Get his number at work, and you call him. (More on this in the next chapter: "Rules of 'The Game.'")

Never, under *any* circumstances, go home with a guy you've just met. I shouldn't have to tell you just how dangerous that can be. You came with your girlfriend—go home with your girlfriend.

Still with me? Very well, we'll assume you've found a possible Playmate. No matter how or where you met, if you see him again, the relationship will probably follow this age-old schedule: first he will suggest meeting for lunch or dinner to get "better acquainted." For this first rendezvous, drive to the appointed restaurant in your car and meet him inside. This way, you have the security of knowing you can leave any time you choose. You may, after dining with him, decide it would be a waste of your time to see him again. If not, a second meeting will probably be for dinner and dancing. By now, a rapport has been established. You should feel comfortable together. Now the physical contact begins, probably in the car. At this point, it's still limited to kissing and petting.

If you have reservations about carrying the relationship to its natural conclusion, sexual intercourse, this is the time to back off. Don't lead him on. Call him at his office the next day and explain that you've decided that it would be best not to continue. Let him down as gently as possible.

The third time is universally considered by men to be "The Night." It may well happen like this:

Together in a dark corner of a cocktail lounge, you are enjoying each other, with the stimulus of the alcohol adding to the seductiveness of the atmosphere. The evening is young; the music conducive to romance, he enfolds you tenderly in his arms. You dance. Fifteen minutes later he whispers in your ear, "Let's get out of here." Unless he has already taken care of the room arrangements, you will have to sit in the car while he registers. You're convinced the desk clerk knows you're not married to each other. Take it from me, a former motel Desk Clerk, the motel doesn't care, as long as you're paying for a double occupancy. So don't worry about it.

So now you're alone together in a motel room. What next? The first time it helps to have some liquor on hand. On the way to the motel, you can suggest stopping to pick up something to drink. But keep it simple. Some drinks require the dexterity of a professional bartender. Pre-mixed canned cocktails are nifty although I prefer Jack Daniels. You can't beat it "straight on-the-rocks" as an instant cure for nervousness.

Fixing a drink gives you something to do until the effect of the alcohol puts you more at ease. Sooner or later, he will take you in his arms, his mouth will find yours and you're on your way to an experience that can change your whole life!

From here on, you're on your own. There just aren't any hard and fast rules. Maybe you will both want to shower first. Maybe he'll want to undress you. One of my Playmates loves to remove all my clothing, piece-by-piece, while driving me wild with desire, smothering me with long, passionate kisses. Undoubtedly, you will eventually end up in bed. The important thing is to let your hair down and enjoy it! Swing with the scene.

Now let's discuss afterwards. Your passion has ebbed. It's time to be thinking about reality again, getting home at a reasonable hour, etc. This is the most awk-ward time of the entire evening, for men as well as women. Nonchalant small talk seems out of place, and an in-depth political discussion is even less appropri-ate. So what do you talk about? How do you handle it? The simple act of switching on the TV can help create a normal, relaxed atmosphere. You can chat about the program you're watching or your favorite shows or some funny movie, while the two of you shower and dress.

By the time you are back in the car heading for home, you will both feel at ease and content.

You have now embarked on an affair!

To find out how to make the most of it, read on . . . !

9

RULES OF "THE GAME"

Every game has rules, and the Adultery Game is no exception. Can you imagine playing baseball or football without knowing the rules? Would you jump into an eight-foot-deep swimming pool if you couldn't swim?

Through the years, through painful trial and error, I have formulated a set of rules that should be adhered to. If you seriously want to play, you should follow them carefully. *Experience is the best teacher and I learned the hard way!* This book will help you, if you heed its advice. You *can* avoid the mistakes I made.

1. *Accept adultery for what it is: an alternative to divorce, a game, a diversion.*

Keep your emotions under absolute control *at all times!* "Impossible," you say? Wrong! It *can* and *must* be done—to protect innocent people. Try to imagine what would happen if you went about killing all the people with whom you were angry—chaos would result: anger is an emotion and it *is* controllable. So is love.

Men learned long ago to draw the line; emotionally, when they play "The Game." They will love you up to a point, but no more. As a Playmate, you are not allowed to trespass on their marriage or their private lives. If the relationship is going to jeopardize their marriage, they will back off, and, if you become too intense, or a threat to their security, they will stop seeing you.

Men *know* what adultery is about, women have to *learn,* usually the hard way. If you think that playing "The Game" will result in a new marriage, *forget it!* It rarely does, so play it for what it's worth and enjoy it. Realism is essential. And, to a novice, the hardest lesson of all!

2. *Never collect souvenirs.*

No matter how tempting, never pick up matches, soap, ash trays, postcards, or anything else from any of the places where you and your Playmate wile away the hours. Picture your husband in search of a stamp, opening your pocketbook and, instead of the stamp, finding several of your souvenirs! How do you explain them to him?

Be especially careful of matchbooks which are very easy to absent-mindedly tuck into a pocket or purse. They could necessitate some fancy footwork and quickly composed explanations.

3. *Never mark a Playmate's body.*

No matter how turned on you are, or how passionate you become, leave his body unscathed. This means no bites, scratches, or other love marks. And don't let him mark you either—but more on that next. Clench your fists, grit your teeth, but *don't* leave tell-tale marks. Remember, he has to go home to his unsuspecting wife. Marks require explanations. Don't put him in jeopardy.

Another common pitfall is lipstick stains. This is a dead giveaway! How can he go home with lipstick on his clothes? But he can't very well go home minus a shirt, can he?

Also, be careful about leaving your scent on him. It stands to reason that if you bathe in perfume, or splash it over every inch of your body, or smear your favorite cream sachet all over you from head to toe, he's going to end up smelling like a rose. You two may not notice it—but his wife will. Get your Playmate to take a shower before going home, if at all possible.

4. *Never let him mark you.*

For equally obvious reasons, don't permit your Playmate to leave tell-tale clues on that beautiful body of yours. How would you ever explain a hickey on your breast? Will your husband believe you if you tell him you bumped into a kitchen cabinet? I wouldn't! Nevertheless, if passion gets the best of you and you find yourself physically marked by your Playmate, get out the old calamine lotion and use the "Unexplained Rash" ruse. Cover the evidence, for your husband's benefit, with lotion and expose yourself as little as possible . . . until the marks disappear. Calamine lotion works great for beard rashes, bites, *and* hickeys! Alas, a lip that is swollen from excessive amorousness is uncoverable. So fake it. Say you bit yourself by accident.

5. *Your Playmate's car: make sure there's no evidence.*

Be extra careful with lipstick-stained cigarettes in his car ash tray. He is supposed to be out on business, remember? How will he explain your cigarette butts to his wife when she uses the car next morning to take the kids to school? Before you leave his car, check for stray bobby pins, gloves, earrings, etc. If his wife found a woman's earring on the floor of their car, she'd never let him out of her sight again!

6. *Watch your own car, too.*

After you use your car for an evening on the town with your Playmate, check to be sure that his cigar butt isn't still in the car ashtray. Or that a cufflink or tie clasp hasn't dropped on the floor.

What if your Playmate inadvertently left his trench coat in the back seat, and your husband discovered it the next morning, and came storming into the house demanding an explanation? As long as there's nothing to identify the coat, you could always say you were supposed to drop it off at the cleaners for a neighbor. But will he *believe* it? That's the question.

7. *Always park discreetly.*

Okay, you've got a date with your Playmate. You'll probably use his car, but where are you going to park yours? Believe it or not, the safest place of all is a hospital parking lot. They're open day and night, or you can leave it in the parking area of an all-night restaurant. Do *not* park in front of your local library!

8. *Never give a stranger your real name or home phone number.*

Not until you *really* know the guy with whom you're getting involved. It *could* spell disaster in the hands of the wrong man! What if after a few dates you decide not to become physically involved, and he retaliates by calling your husband at home some evening for a heart-to-heart talk. I usually use my maiden name; that way they won't find me listed in the phone book.

If and when you meet someone you'd like to see again (and it *will* happen eventually), arrange to call him at work. Once the relationship is firmly established, he will be calling you of course, *but until then you call him!*

9. *Don't entertain at home.*

Under *no* circumstances should you bring a Playmate home. You may be tempted, especially with someone who's very special, but it's too dangerous. I know it's hard to stick to this rule, especially on one of those depressingly cold winter days when you're all alone, and your Playmate calls to say he has a spare hour and would *love* to see you. Don't do it!

What if your husband came home unexpectedly? Don't say it *can't happen*. There's a first time for everything. What if one of your "straight" girlfriends just happens to drop in for coffee, or one of your children suddenly comes home sick?

Even if your husband is out of town and there is positively no chance of him catching you "in the act," again, I say, *"Don't do it!"* It's dangerous emotionally. *You* live with the memory of him, *there,* at *your* kitchen table. Or, worse, the memory of him stretched out in *your* bed, *his* head on *your* pillow. The ghost of his presence in your home can and will make it harder for you to stay objective, cool. It's a lot safer to stick to neutral ground: a motel, a friend's apartment, but not your own home.

This rule works two ways: if his wife is in the hospital, or visiting her family 3,000 miles away, and he's alone at home in her absence baby-sitting for the kids every night, and he invites you over, *don't go!* With his wife safely out of the picture, there may indeed be little chance of getting caught, *but* emotionally it can be extremely damaging. During the time you are apart, living your own lives, you'll find yourself making mental pictures of him, at *his* home, with *his* wife and children.

A very disturbing memory that haunted me for years was of a night I spent in my Playmate Paul's home while his wife was hospitalized. At his insistence, in fact, I even tiptoed in and tucked in his sleeping children, an adorable little boy and girl, curled up like angels with thumbs in mouths. *I* learned the hard way that what you don't know (or see) can't hurt you, while what you do, can.

10. *Never recognize a Playmate if you're with your husband.*

If you are out shopping with your husband or out on the town, and you unexpectedly meet a Playmate, past or present, *never* show it. This is a point you should be sure to get across to all your Playmates, right at the start. Can you envision your husband's reaction if some strange man comes up to you and says, "Cheryl! Hi! How are you? How are you enjoying your night-school course this semester?" If such a situation does arise, just reply, "Oh, fine," and keep walking. *Don't* introduce him to your husband and *don't* linger. When he's safely out of earshot, explain to your husband that he's the husband of one of the women in your night school course, and that you didn't introduce him because you couldn't remember his name.

11. *He should pay his fair share.*

It's wise, early in the game, to insist that your Playmate pay your taxi and baby-sitters (if you have to hire one to go out with him). He should also pay for your gas if you wind up using your car. After all, you incurred these expenses because of him. This rule especially applies to daytime meetings, when you slip away for a few hours without your husband even knowing you've stepped out.

12. *If you're with your husband, stay away from those "special places."*

Both you and your Playmate should avoid the places that you routinely visit with your spouses. If not, you may run into problems. For instance, one time when my husband decided to take me out for a night of dining and dancing on the town for my birthday, he chose a new restaurant that my Playmate and I considered "our" place. I had no excuse for not wanting to go there and since he had already made the reservations, I had no choice but to go, hoping and praying that the waiters, who knew my Playmate and I by first name, would cool it. Things went well, until after dinner, when the owner of the restaurant just happened to walk by, recognized me, stopped at our table: "Hi, how's Lee?" (my current Playmate). My mind raced. As casually as possible, I answered, "Oh, *she's* fine." After the owner left, I explained that Lee was a girl I bowled with, and that this guy bowled, too, which is how he knew me. Whew!

If my Playmate's name had been George? I would have said, "You've got me confused with someone else." Remember, in a situation like this, *lie*. Stay cool and bluff your way out!

13. *Never put anything incriminating in writing.*

This is a common mistake of women who play "The Game." They write long and emotional letters and poems, or send those witty one-line greeting cards, like: "Let's get something straight between us," to a Playmate at his office. My advice? Forget love sonnets and passionate dissertations—you are *not* Elizabeth Barrett Browning!

If some deep need impels you to express yourself, then at least *type* your letters. Never sign your name. Don't worry, your Playmate will know who the sender is!

Letters from you to him, in your own hand, and signed by you, could prove extremely detrimental, *later*. Imagine what choice evidence his wife would have if she inadvertently stumbled upon a stack of passionate love letters with your name on them!

91

If you are the type to write poetry about your Playmates or keep a secret diary filled with intimate details, for your own protection keep such incriminating mementos in a safe place, well hidden. Rent a safe deposit box or lock it up in your desk at the office. Better still, don't write down anything incriminating. A suspicious husband won't hesitate to turn the house upside-down while you're out if he knows you are the type to write poetry or keep a diary.

14. *Always remember birth control.*

Never leave it up to your Playmate. Get fitted for a diaphragm, an intra-uterine device (loop or I.U.D.) or take The Pill. In the heat of passion, contraception is surely the *last* thing either of you are thinking about, but it will be the *first* thing later on, when you've cooled off a bit.

I always feel safer at the start of a new affair if my Playmate uses a condom, because venereal diseases have reached epidemic proportions. As the affair progresses and you're more sure of your Playmate's habits, you can skip the condom bit. If you use a diaphragm at home, buy two! Keep one in the regular spot at home and carry the other at all times, tucked discreetly inside your cosmetic bag inside your pocketbook. This way, you're always prepared. If some night when you're absent from home, your husband gets suspicious and decides to check, he will find your diaphragm in its usual place. This will reassure him.

Suppose you meet a man who claims to have had a vasectomy. *He could be lying* . . . so take your normal precautions. Remember, if *he's* not telling the truth, *you* get pregnant, not him. The responsibility for birth control is yours, first, last and always!

15. *Let your Playmate go gracefully.*

If your Playmate, whom you consider the great love

of your life, turns to you some evening and says, "I think it would be best if we cooled it for awhile," *don't flip!* Accept the inevitable and let him walk out of your life without a nasty scene. You can't force him to keep on seeing you. He "owes" you nothing, and the end of an affair is *not* the end of the world!

If you get involved in a one-sided relationship, and find yourself all strung out over a Playmate, there is only one logical course of action: *STOP SEEING HIM!* Let him go, before he breaks off with you. You *can* live without him. You *will* survive, and a clean break, especially one initiated by you, is the least painful.

16. *Never call your Playmate at his home.*

This rule should *not* be broken under any circumstances. What if his wife picked up the extension? If he lives out of town, his phone number will show up as a toll call on your phone bill. No matter how important it is that you get in touch with him, *never* call him at home! Let's suppose you have a date to meet him at the usual place at 8:00 PM and then all hell breaks loose at your house and you can't get out. If you were planning to meet him at a bar or restaurant, at 8:05 PM, call him there and have him paged, or leave a cryptic message—"Meeting for this evening cancelled" —and sign it with your husband's first name and your maiden name. Don't worry—he'll get the message.

You would be wise if you refrained from calling him at work, too, unless he has asked you to, or you have a pressing reason. This could be construed as "pushing," or "chasing," or "pressuring," all of which are *no's*. If you do call him at work, it might be wise to have it appear as a business call rather than a personal one. Many employers frown on employees receiving personal phone calls.

17. *Never give your Playmate your picture, and don't accept his.*

One picture is worth a thousand words, remember that! It is dangerous for you to exchange pictures and it could spell disaster if you have your picture taken together and each of you keep a copy.

I made this mistake and the results were dire. One summer night a Playmate and I went to an amusement park, ate cotton candy and hot dogs, rode on the roller coaster, etc. We also went into the Penny Arcade and on the spur of the moment decided to have our pictures taken together in one of those "four poses for 50¢" booths. Afterwards, we both took two of the pictures. I was wise enough to hide mine in a safe place, but he unthinkingly tucked his copies in his jacket pocket and forgot all about them—and his wife found them there the next day! She had suspected that he was playing "The Game." Now she knew for sure! A good detective could have tracked me down if she had decided to go all the way and sue for a divorce. Luckily, my Playmate talked her out of it by telling her that he had gotten drunk one night—after an argument with her at home—and picked me up in a bar and that he didn't even remember my name. His wife believed him! Now when I'm with a Playmate I avoid cameras like the plague.

18. *Never admit to prior affairs.*

The fastest way to dampen a Playmate's ardor is to start spouting off about your experiences with former Playmates. The best policy is to let each new Playmate think that this affair is your first. Men need the illusion of being the first illicit sex partner you have had. (Because of *them* you are willing to commit the cardinal sin of adultery! *Wow!*)

19. *Never talk disparagingly of your husband or men in general to a Playmate.*

Another mistake a woman can make is to put down her husband and men in general. Don't start in about what a clod you are married to. Just don't say anything.

I have found that most Playmates complain only about their wives' lack of interest in sex; they will usually state that she is an excellent mother, a competent housekeeper and a good cook. Strange as it may seem, most of my Playmates are curious about my husband's sexual prowess and "how many inches" he is endowed with! If you're smart, you won't tell! Men are curious about how they stack up against a rival. They wonder what the "norm" is. But size means very little in terms of your enjoyment of sex. It's not how much he has, but the way he uses it that counts.

20. *Never bore a Playmate with your household, family or health problems.*

Don't misconstrue this rule. When you're having a long-term affair with someone, it will be normal for you at times to mention your home life: "Our cellar is flooded with water." "The baby fell and had to have five stitches in her chin," or, "I've got to enter the hospital for some routine tests." *But,* your Playmate will be bored stiff if you limit your conversations *only* to the nitty-gritty day-to-day problems you face. He gets enough of this at home from his wife.

21. *Never accept gifts from your Playmate.*

Well, maybe a very small gift. But remember that you may have to explain how you got it. It's conceivable that you bought yourself a bottle of Chanel No. 5, but your husband knows you can't afford a mink stole —or a cashmere bathrobe—or a complete set of Pucci underwear—or a Cartier watch.

22. *Use tact when breaking off with a Playmate.*

You've been having an affair but have gradually lost interest. You'd like to have this Playmate for a friend now instead of a lover, or maybe you want to end the relationship completely, especially if you sense that he's getting over-involved emotionally. Tact is essential; there's no need to destroy his ego in the process of ending the relationship. It's best to part friends, if possible.

When you want to end an affair, here are a few simple ways to do so:

Tell him that your husband is getting suspicious so you've got to cool it for a while; having set the stage, cool it permanently.

Every time he calls, come up with a plausible excuse for not seeing him. For example, say you have a sick child, house guests, you are sick yourself with a disease—like mononucleosis—that takes months of bed rest for recovery.

Tell him that you just can't cope with the affair emotionally; you've become over-involved. This should scare him off!

And if all else fails, tell him that you and your husband have decided to see a marriage counselor!

23. *Never pry into your Playmate's personal affairs.*

Women are by nature curious creatures, and often try to learn more about a Playmate's wife, children and business than is necessary or smart. As I've stated before, what you don't know won't hurt you, and besides, it's none of your business what his yearly salary is, how much he paid for his home, or how he spends his time when he's apart from you! Never "pump" him about his wife: her age, what she looks like, how she responds to him sexually, etc. Often he'll volunteer personal information about his home life or business pressures: my eight-year-old son is doing poorly in second grade, or my wife joined a health spa so I'm free every Wednesday night, or I'm being considered for a promotion. Listen. Praise. But don't PRY!

10

PLAYMATES

Generally speaking, whether you meet them in a bar, at the office, or while taking a night school course in "Business Management," all prospective Playmates fall into definite, easy-to-assign categories, etc. Their largest common denominator is their interest in "playing."

After some practical experience, you will become an expert at identifying most of the various Playmate types in five minutes—or less. The following examples of types and their goals are classic. Study them well. This guide will save you invaluable time and energy.

The Hard Sell

"I'm great in bed, baby!"

This type verbally comes on strong, literally selling himself like a product. "What have we got to lose?" "We only live once." "You've never had it until you've had it with me." "I can take care of you. I'm just what you need." He ranges in age from 21, and is usually involved in dealing directly with the public. He's neatly dressed, drives a big car, is intelligent, self-assured, a fantastic dancer, and emotionally detached. He feels that *every* woman can be made and is confident of his ability to prove it. He is unusually proud of his sexual proficiency, and rightly so, and often has a tendency to brag about his past conquests. His line is: "I love my wife, but oh you kid!" Sometimes he uses reverse psychology: "What's the matter? You don't like me?" and you will find yourself on the defensive. Conquest is the name of his game. He will have an affair with you until he tires of you sexually; then he will let you down gently. A soft-hearted "Hard Sell" will be a valuable asset as a friend, after your affair is over.

My first introduction to the "Hard Sell" was unexpected—as usual! A girlfriend and I decided to stop by a local restaurant for pizza and beer after an especially interesting lecture we had attended. There we were, sipping beer and having a lively discussion about the lecture: "ESP—A Fantasy or Reality?", when a strange man pulled up a chair and joined us! What a nerve, I thought. Then my girlfriend burst out laughing and introduced us. Lee was her hairdresser, a guy she had known for years, but because he just wasn't her type their relationship remained purely platonic.

Well, Lee moved in on me—and fast! Five minutes after we met he came right to the point: "You're beautiful. How about dinner tomorrow, or whenever you're free? I *must* see you again!"

My girlfriend and I were amused by the big play, and we teased him mercilessly for coming on so strong. Without saying anything that could be considered in bad taste, he let us both know he was a "super-stud" . . . and proud of it! He must have known at least eighty percent of the women in the place, all of whom stopped by our table to fawn over him. He took it all with complete calm, but his utter lack of interest, his outright boredom showed clearly. A man like this can have his pick—and suddenly I was the one!

Flattered and amused by his interest, I *did* go out to dinner with him the following week. We spent a very pleasant evening dining, dancing and talking. I discovered that he underplayed his intelligence, that he

99

had more depth than I had originally thought. We had an affair that lasted several months, and then gradually our relationship changed to one of friendship. And it's quite nice to have a friend who, on five minutes notice, will squeeze me in between regular appointments when I look like a disaster area and have less than one hour to get my hair together.

The Soft Sell

"Whatever you want, honey, just as long as I score."

This one's basically a con artist, very soft spoken, a pro at persuasion. From him you'll hear: "You're fantastic, one in a million." And even "I love you." Anything to make and keep you.

Exceptionally intelligent, he can talk the birds out of the trees. So beware! He's very selective, though he won't push. Usually conservative and business-like in his dress (no "bell-bottoms" for this guy), he's over thirty-five, drives a new car and usually doesn't dance too well. His line consists of: "I am unhappily married but have serious financial and moral obligations that make divorce impossible." He wants long-term affairs, and will be a sympathetic friend when it's over.

The Male Animal

Young or old, this man radiates pure animal magnetism and has a dynamic personality. He is the male "sex symbol." He doesn't have to pursue women, they pursue him and will do anything to attract his attention—ask him to dance, light his cigarettes—anything.

He's easy to spot—his virility can be felt across a crowded room. He attracts women like crumbs attract ants. Always fashionably dressed, he has a quick wit and is an expert at handling people of all ages, *especially* women. Like a chameleon, he fits in anywhere.

He shies away from any deep, lasting emotional involvement because it can become "so, you know, heavy." He's looking for affairs with "no strings." His terms, or not at all. He is very selective about the women he sleeps with and will be faithful to you while your affair lasts, but you will only be one of many he's had and you'd be wise never to forget this fact. He is married, frequently to a frigid woman, but plans no change of status, usually because of children. You will have *great* sex with him . . . until he becomes bored and moves on. But you can probably remain friends.

Anyway, beware: this kind of man is easy to get hooked on!

Never Been Married

"Forbidden fruit is always sweetest."

He's usually in his late twenties or early thirties, a swinger in every sense of the word! Your wedding ring means "safe" to him and he figures that you're simply looking for a change of pace. He wears the newest fashions and knows the latest dances. He has an apartment of his own in which to entertain and will usually prefer spending the evenings there with you, sipping wine, digging the stereo, making love. Because you're married, he won't take you too seriously, but an affair *is* possible . . . that is, until he meets a single girl to marry or live with.

Mr. Put-on

"I have to keep up my image, but I don't really want to play."

Normally found in offices, this type talks a big game, may proposition you openly, but doesn't really want to play. He's *all* talk and no action. He may take you out to lunch, but never cocktails after work. Call his bluff, and he'll back down fast. He likes to come on strong, to play the swinger, but this Don Juan's a phony. Secretly he's afraid that he won't measure up in bed.

I met one of these characters at a local supermarket once. He was about forty, medium height, blond, dark eyed and very attractive (and he knew it, too). He was manager of the meat department and every time I approached the meat section he'd rush forward to greet me. "And how are you today?" he'd say. "My, that outfit looks stunning on you!" etc. He always had a compliment, but gradually his tone changed. I began to hear remarks like: "I really dig your legs!" And, "Those big, brown eyes really turn me on." As a bonus, he'd cut my meat to order, even throwing in a couple of extra pork chops or chicken breasts, for free.

One afternoon, as he stood behind the counter as usual, he looked me in the eye and said: "You're such a turn-on, I bet you keep your husband in a constant state of exhaustion!" Then and there, I turned the tables and called his bluff: "How'd you like to find out for yourself? Just name the time and place." I thought he'd have a heart attack right on the spot! Silently, he turned and walked quickly away. He now avoids me like the plague.

Past His Prime

"I'm in Heaven just being near a beautiful young woman like you."

This man is mainly seeking to prop up a sagging ego. He is usually "over-the-hill" physically and sexually. For him it's now or never. He needs the illusion of feeling desirable to a woman—*any* woman, but preferably one who's under forty. Usually a true gentleman, he will be grateful for any attention or affection you might give. You'll visit the more sedate restaurants with six-course dinners, complemented by several rare vintage wines! An affair with him will be brief. After all, he can't keep it up *indefinitely!*

Having lunch alone one afternoon in a quiet restaurant, I was approached by a well-dressed, distinguished-looking man of about sixty who inquired as nonchalantly as possible, "Haven't we met some place before?" Now *really!* That line went out with bustles! I almost burst out laughing, but in order not to embarrass him I just shook my head and said that I didn't think so.

He just stood, staring down at me, not knowing what to say or do next. Since I had finished the main course, I asked him if he'd like to join me for coffee. He sat down, beaming with pleasure. We introduced ourselves (his name was Graham). I stressed the "Mrs." I mean, he was old enough to be my father! After lunch, he gave me his card and almost begged me to call him and have lunch some time soon.

One dreary, rainy day, I felt the walls closing in so I gave Graham a call and we met an hour later for lunch. Lunch was in the private dining room of the Lawyers' Club. He introduced me to his old cronies. Oh, and did their envy of Graham ever show! A man of his age with a girlfriend like her! Graham really blew their minds! We never did have an affair, although we saw each other occasionally until, with his wife, he moved to a retirement home in Florida.

The Grabber

"Hey, baby, you've got a great little body there. C'mon, let me touch it—what's it cost you?"

103

This type is found everywhere. He's all hands, a turn-off, unless you enjoy being pawed!

I first came across "The Grabber" in a bar. He was partly looped, good-looking and well-dressed, but crass! A clod with absolutely no finesse. Uninvited, he sat down at my table, told a dirty joke I didn't want to hear and generally was utterly crude, grabbing any part of me he could get hold of. One arm went around my shoulders "accidentally" brushing up against my breast, the other hand was under the table . . . trying! I was frantically gesturing to get the waitress's attention. She saw what was happening and sent the manager over to rescue me. As they escorted "The Grabber" from my table and out the nearest door, he made some pretty crude remarks in a voice that could be heard across the room.

The Bomb-out

"I was really *going to* swing, but the alcohol hit me first and I blew it."

This one might have made a great Playmate, but you'll never know. The booze has taken care of *that!* He's well-dressed, sophisticated, and oozing self-confidence. If he approaches, he'll sit down and calmly start a conversation, then promptly pass out, either falling on the table in front of him, or back in his chair! Call the waitress and ask her to get rid of *"it."* Too bad; you didn't even get his name.

The Good-Time Charlie

"I need a strange piece of ass, but I can't say I love you."

This guy is easy to spot because of his boyish charm.

He can be any age, but looks and acts years younger than he really is. He loves a good time and likes to bring laughter and fun wherever he goes. He wears the latest styles, usually doesn't dance too well but *is* willing to try, has a winning smile, is charming and unsophisticated and very likable.

He doesn't drive the flashiest car and usually isn't the high-paid executive or doctor/lawyer type. He can be very appealing, though, because he has a great sense of humor. Anything goes when you're out with him. He's *not* too cool to ask the band to play your favorite song every fifteen minutes. But first and foremost, he is looking for a willing sex partner. No future with this type. Just out on the town to find a new bed-mate. The bar is his natural habitat; one-night stands, his specialty. He is permanently married but occasionally seeking a change of pace. The Good-Time Charlie's classic line? "Sex and love are two different things."

The Man-About-Town

"I have the best of everything, the cream of the crop is mine for the asking."

Usually over forty, self-employed, intelligent, *ultra*-sophisticated, and cool, this one can "take 'em or leave 'em." His conversation centers around himself, for he is his own biggest fan. A perfect gentleman at all times, at all costs, women just don't faze him. He can have his choice, he expects adoration. Married, well-off, handsome, debonair, he is perfection personified. Or so *he* thinks!

Unless *you* are the one-in-a-million, this guy won't play—he figures it's a waste of *his* time!

"I've read all the best pornography and now I want to *do* it all!"

Almost always over forty, a well-established businessman who can and does spend money like water to make up for a mediocre appearance and dish-water personality, this type goes in for far-out sexual fantasizing and accepts the unrealistic concepts of sex portrayed in pornography. He wants to experience it all before it's too late.

In his company you will be wined and dined royally, and because of feelings of inadequacy, he will take his time leading up to the big score. Not an avid conversationalist, insecure, he can't wait to get you in bed, where *anything goes!* You'll strike out before he's given you a fair change—no woman can live up to his adolescent fantasies. Good luck if you get involved with this type!

The Gigolo

"My body is my living. If you want to play, you have to pay."

The gigolo, although rare, *does* exist. Because his body is his stock-in-trade, he's always handsome, well-dressed, polished, and confident. He *sells* his physical services—he's a pro. He will have an affair with you for a price, although sometimes he'll take on a woman just because she appeals to him. He preys on the old and the lonely—divorcees, widows, old maids.

You can spot him in a minute: he heads right for the women over forty-five, who wistfully watch the dancing, hoping someone, *anyone,* will ask *them.* Like a computer, the gigolo sizes them up—expensive clothes or rags, fake jewelry or real—and then he moves in.

I had a gigolo for a lover once who had played "The Establishment Game," but then dropped out and decided to sell his body instead of his brains!

The Wise Kid

"I've never been turned on like this before."

This type ranges in age from eighteen to twenty-two, is usually in college, single, a familiar face. He could be a neighbor's son, or maybe the kid who cuts the grass or shovels the snow—he's someone you see regularly. Although he never actually makes a pass, his infatuation is obvious. He's shy all right, but his eyes give him away. He thinks you're terrific . . . even though you're probably ten or fifteen years older than he is.

Make no mistake about it: the boy has been around sexually. The younger generation is pretty advanced these days. He is probably *more* experienced than a mature man.

The Platonic Friend

"Adultery is not my game—friendship is."

He's over forty, neatly dressed, intelligent, with a heart of gold. Usually a professional traveler on an expense account, his motto is "eat, drink, and be merry." With *one* exception: *no messing around!* He could be straight for moral reasons, a potency problem; or he may possibly be a latent homosexual who still hasn't come out of the closet. In any event, you can have a lot of fun with this guy.

John is a platonic friend. We met one night in the lounge of the motel where he and his boss George were staying. When it was time to leave, John asked me for my phone number, and I broke my rule and gave it to him. Six weeks later he had to check up on a job in our area and gave me a call. We had dinner together, and danced our legs off. After that, we went on meeting for some months. He'd call me the day before he was scheduled to be in town, which gave me time to come up with an airtight alibi. We'd talk and eat and drink and dance, but *no* sex.

I couldn't figure it out! What was wrong with me? John had never even made a pass, although he had kissed me a few times. So, one night I finally asked him what was wrong, and he said that he was happily married and didn't approve of adultery—yet here we were, together every time he hit town! What a contradiction!

Frankly, I didn't believe him, so the next time business brought him to my area and we made arrangements to get together as usual, I decided to determine the truth for myself. I used the "shopping excuse," meeting John at 4:00 PM for an early drink and dinner. As we sat in the lounge of our favorite restaurant waiting for a table, I rapidly consumed three Black Russians and pretended to be totally smashed. Since John couldn't take me home in this condition and since it was also only 5:00 PM, he took me to his motel room to sober me up. He instructed me to take a cold shower; I climbed naked into bed, and when he returned with the coffee, I suggested he join me. He stripped and soon we were in each others' arms, kissing and petting heavily. He made love to me almost automatically, dispassionately until we both reached orgasm. We drank coffee sitting up in bed, and a short while later the love-play began again. But it was one-sided: he took my hand and showed me what he wanted done to his body, but he didn't touch or fondle me. Judging by the hardness of his erection, I assumed he was ready for sexual intercourse again, and he accommodated me—until I reached my climax; then I had to give him a "blow job" for him to make it!

We left the motel shortly after and had a late dinner. I returned home full of unanswered questions. His lack of passion disturbed me. Was it due to a guilty conscience, his age, a potency problem, or because he was a latent homosexual? I'll never know! But we remain friends and I look forward to his visits. Needless to say, we now stay *out* of bed!

The Childhood Friend

"I liked her as a child; I loved her as a woman."

He could be a boy you were madly in love with in high school, or the boy next door, or an old friend of the family who is about your age. Perhaps your families were friends. Or he could have been one of your teachers, your older brother's or sister's friend, someone from your past. Time has passed; you've both married, and, of course, lost contact with each other. Then, after many years, you meet again, perhaps at a high school or college reunion, or an old home town get-together. If you hit it off, an affair could result, and since you're friends already, it should be lots of fun!

Poor Me, I've Got Problems!

"I'm lost, sad, insecure. I want my mommy."

Typical sad sack. You can spot him in a minute in any bar. He sits alone, hunched over his drink, looking extremely troubled. Naturally when he invites you to dance or buys you a drink, you're certain to ask if anything is the matter, because he looks as if he just lost his best friend; and that's his angle. His face has a perpetually troubled look; there is an aura of sadness around him. You'll find yourself listening to his problems, and, believe me, he'll have plenty—his wife, job, children, the whole world!

He is a "loser." Unrealistically, he blames everyone *except* himself for his problems. He will spend money like water as long as you hold his hand and sympathize and act as his crying towel. If you have an affair with him, you won't be his mistress, you'll be his substitute *mother!* The wife he has at home is usually "the boss." Hen-pecked is the word for him, in fact. This type tends to get over-involved emotionally and can be extremely demanding and possessive. Of average intelligence, he is an introvert who truly *needs* a friend.

Straight—Won't Play

"I have what I want. I was tempted for a moment, but it's really not worth the effort."

This type of guy is fairly common. He's usually a very successful businessman, engineer, college professor, doctor—a professional man. He's probably at least thirty-five, "squarely" dressed, well-read, and morally straight. Basically happy at home in his comfortable rut, he was most likely in the bar because he had an *argument* with his wife (these gentlemen never *fight!*). He will buy you a drink or dance with you, but it ends there, finished before it ever got started. Simply having an illicit drink or dance with a strange, attractive, desirable woman is enough to inflate his ego; then he goes home to his dull wife and fantasizes! This type is usually unable to cope with a casual affair; he can't handle it, so unless he decides to start a whole new life, he just won't play! It's *all* or nothing with him. What a waste!

Male Tramp

"Any broad is a place to put it."

This type can be any age, in any profession, from a machine operator to an airline pilot. As the evening progresses, he will come right to the point: sex. He can be quite insistent, especially if he has spent the whole evening with you. He thinks you "owe" him a screw. If you make it crystal clear early in the evening that you have no intention of jumping into the nearest bed with him, he'll usually move on to another prospect. He is incapable of emotion. To him, love is just a four-letter word.

Playboys

"The world is my oyster; I want variety in women. In return, I offer the world."

These "jet setters" are usually over forty—self-made, self-employed "wheeler-dealers." They are well-set financially. What they lack in physical appeal, they make up for by wining and dining you like a queen. With them you won't eat at the local diner; it's the best place in town for them, *always*. Cheap, out-of-town motels are just not his speed; it's the biggest and the best for him—with room service, naturally, for intimate dinners and champagne for two! They always go "first class," and so will you. They are usually kind, and no pressure will be applied if you date them a few times and then decide not to sleep with them. These guys can be fun to be with, and you could end up good friends. Don't expect marriage, though; they have a middle-aged wife at home, clinging like ivy.

The Teaser

"I get my kicks listening to other people's problems, especially sexual ones. I'm afraid of involvement, but am often tempted."

He deals on a one-to-one basis with people in general, but especially women. He might be a personnel interviewer, beautician, doctor, lawyer, bartender. Whatever he does, warmth and sincerity are his trademarks. He is usually middle-aged, and what he may lack in physical appeal, he makes up for with personality. You will instantly feel empathy with him. He's married, basically straight, but gets his kicks and boosts his ego by playing come-on games. His female counterpart is the "Cock Teaser." It's permissible to kiss and pet and feel around a little, but he won't go all the way; he uses women only as ego-builders. Let's face it—most women *love* to talk, especially about themselves, and he's a perfect listener. To get himself off the hook, he'll tell you that *he* can't hack an affair, emotionally—after doing everything *but* making love to you!

Several years ago as a newcomer to the community, I had to locate a new doctor for my family. Thumbing through the Yellow Pages, I picked a physician at random, and called his office for an appointment; luckily, he was accepting new patients. During my initial examination, the doctor discovered that my blood pressure was elevated and scheduled monthly check-ups for me. Over the years, my blood pressure continued to fluctuate, and it became a pleasant routine to visit Dr. J's comfortable and pleasant office each month. He was kind and compassionate and never failed to put me at ease.

Any physician will admit that a great deal of his time is taken up with patients whose ailments are psychosomatic—the bored housewife, the lonely elderly person, the neurotic. Dr. J's forte was to listen sympathetically, to be concerned and to help, if possible.

As the years passed, we got to know each other well. My secret life came unexpectedly to light during a routine visit when my blood pressure was higher than usual and Dr. J. wanted to know *why*. I was upset and found myself telling him about a recent involvement in which I had over-extended myself emotionally and had abruptly ended the affair. Dr. J gave me a pep talk, rebuilt my confidence and then confessed his interest in me. He suggested that I drop by his office on Saturday—after office hours. In shock and anticipation, I agreed to a 2:00 PM meeting. I couldn't believe that *he* played "The Game!"

When I arrived, Dr. J called: "Come in," and closed the inner office door. I sat in my usual chair beside the desk as we discussed a liaison. Finally he came out from behind the desk. Pulling an armchair alongside mine, he took my hand, patted it, and began working his way up. Love play in this position wasn't easy—the arms of the captains' chairs were in the way! He finally got his arm around me and began kissing me. I was responding when—the phone rang!

"Dr. J," he said as he adjusted his glasses and clothing. Frantically, I tried to straighten my own attire. "Yes, I see," he said. "I'll be right over." He replaced the phone and turned to me: "One of my patients at a convalescent home is in critical condition. I have to leave immediately."

"Of course. I understand," I mumbled. As I left, he kissed me quickly and said, "I'll call soon."

Two days later, he did call. I was so glad to hear his voice that his words almost didn't register. "I've decided

113

that we really shouldn't see each other. *I* can't handle the situation emotionally. And I think it best that you find a new doctor."

I couldn't believe it! "But that's ridiculous! There's no reason why our friendship can't continue. . . ."

"No. It would just be setting the stage—we'd never keep it that way. It wouldn't work. I'm sorry, my dear, but try to understand."

I said goodbye, and that I understood. And I did understand—all too well! It was clear that he got his sexual kicks from leading women on and then backing off.

I had several more appointments with him before I found a new doctor. Each time I left the waiting room I noticed an increasing number of attractive female patients—and I wondered how many of them would be asked in for that special Saturday afternoon appointment!

Divorced Men (No. 1)

"To tell the truth, I need a housekeeper."

This guy is usually a loner. He can be any age, any occupation. He will brag that he is divorced, his stock line being, "My wife was no good, so I divorced her." Don't believe it! *She* probably threw him out! This one is very interested in marriage, providing you have only one or two children (preferably grown). What he needs is a place to hang his hat and someone to cook his meals and do his laundry. He can become a big problem, by pushing too hard. Finding a new wife is his chief goal.

"I'm afraid of women. I'm supposed to be a swinger, but old habits cling. I can handle only one woman at a time."

This one is also solitary, remote, and frightened by any deeply emotional situation; shy, he's been traumatized by divorce. He feels responsible for the failure of his marriage, and is terrified of becoming *involved* again. He will probably head for a very young chick who poses no challenge or threat to him. He is incapable of handling more than one relationship at a time. With his cautious, hesitant ways, he's just what you don't need—a lost cause!

The Traveling Man

"I'm lonely, bored; I'd be thrilled to have your company."

This guy is usually a salesman or a company representative in his late thirties or early forties, with a family in some other state. He's all alone in the big city and will actively seek female companionship, a "home-away-from-home." He will sometimes risk asking out a gal who works for one of the companies he visits, or the girl at the desk of the motel where he is staying, but usually he takes "the bar route." He looks for long-term relationships so that the next time he's in town, he'll have something to do, someone to call. His line is "I'm unhappily married but can't get a divorce because my wife won't let me go without taking the house, the car, and most of my salary." You'll live high on the hog with him; he's on an expense account.

The Novice

"I seek what I once felt in my youth: passion, romance, and *joie de vivre!*"

A fantastic find! He's a stable family man out for some of that action he's always heard about. He's new at playing "The Game," and is still innocent, open and warm. He's usually over thirty, neatly dressed, intelligent, and very considerate. He doesn't have a line; in fact, he doesn't quite know what to say or do with a strange woman. His inexperience is obvious; he is very reserved and unsure of himself, and it will take several dates before he gets enough nerve to seduce you. Since this is his first time out, he may even experience some difficulty in bed, because of guilt feelings. Give him time. Remember, *you* are the first woman he has become involved with in many years. Treat him gently— he's worth his weight in gold.

The Old Hippie

"Come fly with me."

When you think of a hippie, you probably picture a young guy with long hair, sloppy clothes, not very clean, "doing his own thing, man." The Old Hippie is pretty much the same: long hair, blue jeans, boots. On closer observation, you see that he isn't young at all, he's trying to be. He's middle-aged and anti-Establishment, naturally. Look closer at the gray hair, the creased face, the hard eyes—you'll find this is an *old* hippie.

If you do happen to connect with one of these guys, I guarantee you won't need more than one meeting to find out you've got nothing in common! He'll sneer at your "middle-class materialism" and you'll be uncomfortable in the lotus position, and probably not too crazy about Crunchy Granola.

The Great Pretender

"I'm a pillar of the community. Do you think they'll take your word against mine?"

He's found in every community, large or small. Born, bred and raised in the area, he's inherited a thriving business and is a well-known, respectable, solid citizen.

I'd known Harold for some time. The head of a large lumber company and also involved in other local enterprises, he was a pillar of the community, a trusted, respected businessman. When I was working at the Motor Inn, Harold would stop by occasionally to see my boss, the owner. He always treated me with the utmost respect and politeness.

One day I stopped in at a local lounge after an exhausting day of job interviews. I was uptight and needed to unwind before facing the confusion waiting for me at home. I was relaxing at a table, looking at no one, when Harold, who had been at the bar, came over, having recognized me from the days at the Inn. A nice-looking man in his early forties with a baby face and kind, trustworthy eyes, I never for a moment doubted his intentions. I thought of him as a real friend. Sitting at my table, Harold and I began to chat about this and that, the old days at the Inn. He insisted on ordering for me—he had an account at the lounge. I still wonder what was in that drink.

As it was getting close to 6:00 PM, I said I had to leave. We were just out the front door when he said, "My car is parked right here in front. Let's take a short ride, then I'll bring you back. I want to talk to you about a problem."

"But Harold, I have to get home. I mustn't be late."

117

"Just a short little drive; I promise." I got into his deluxe Cadillac. As we cruised along, Harold told me that he'd had a heart attack and had become quite insecure; he felt he was developing an impotency problem. I told him that this was very common after an attack and was most likely due to fears about the condition of his heart. We veered off the main road onto a wooded and deserted lane. "Harry, what are we doing *here?* What's going on?" Pulling the car to a stop, he shut off the ignition and pulled me to him. I was in utter panic and shock. *Not Harold, of all people.* I reasoned, pushed, fought him off. In a daze I heard, "You can help me. I know you can." He was pushing my face into his lap. Oh no, he was exposed and wanted me to. . . . I fought with all my strength and got loose, half suffocated. I crawled out the door, crying. "Harold, I never thought you'd act like this. You've known me so long. How *could* you?" He said he was very sorry, and took me straight back to the parking lot at the lounge. I was too emotionally drained to argue. It was futile, anyway.

As I jumped out the car door, Harold called, "I'll phone you soon." I never looked back. Of course, he never called or apologized. I knew it was hopeless to report the "incident"; no one would have believed my story. I could hardly believe it myself. After all, this was the same "gentleman" who, with his wife, went to President Nixon's 1973 Inaugural Ball.

The Alcoholic

"One little drink leads to another and another, and another. I mean well, but a woman who meets me ends up in hell."

This type bears no distinguishing marks. He can be any man, anywhere, anytime. He may consider himself

118

a "social" drinker and not an alcoholic. There are millions of these men in the United States. Some will not admit their problem, others aren't even aware of it as such. I've met several alcoholics, but haven't always immediately seen their problem. One man I met told me his problems at once, but I chose to think he was exaggerating. That's how I got entangled.

Not long ago, my husband and I got into a hassle and I left the house to cool off. As I drove aimlessly around, I passed a lounge where I'd heard cocktail waitresses were needed. What the hell, I thought, I'll see about a job, cocktail waitresses make more than office workers, or at least I'll have a drink.

It was the manager's night off, but still tense and angry from the fight, I decided to have a drink, anyway. I ordered a Manhattan. There were two men at the bar. The older man began to talk. Chatting about some friends' vacation trip to Venezuela, I heard the tall, handsome stranger to my left say, "I spent several months there." Soon, Richie and I were engrossed in discussion of the country, the people, etc. He was so sweet, so warm. I still remember the way he said, "Ease up on the drinking, unless you're used to belting down Manhattans that fast." I guess he was amused at my obvious inability to hold my own with the drinking group.

Richie told me he was being sued for divorce and had been living in motels and on the road for weeks since the papers were served. He was a service engineer for a large defense firm and did a good deal of traveling. Quietly, he told me he was an alcoholic and that this was his second marriage "on the rocks." He was the father of five children, the stepfather of two. It was hard to believe; he looked only about thirty. Maybe because I was getting bombed myself, or maybe because I didn't want to accept what he was saying, I passed over his words: "I'm an alcoholic; I've destroyed two

119

women." Later, he took me for coffee to sober me up for my trip home.

So warm, so friendly, not pushing for sex, Richie brought out the mother in me. I felt so sorry for him, I spent a great deal of time and emotional energy finding him an apartment and a lawyer, trying to help him face and solve his alcohol problems; I was almost obsessed with getting him on his feet again. But his drinking persisted, despite all my efforts. Then I realized that Richie wasn't interested in *me;* he only wanted the attention of a mother figure focused on him. Richie didn't want to be cured of his alcohol problem, because he lacked the motivation to try.

Need I tell you that my rehabilitation program was a failure? Richie went back to his wife and now he's *her* problem.

11

WHAT PLAYMATES WANT

Let's get down to brass tacks. Without exception, *all* of the men I have known had one thing in common. Every one complained either that his wife was cold and indifferent to sex, or that she just didn't turn him on anymore. Instead of warm responsiveness, all they hear is:

"I'm too tired tonight."

"Hurry up and get it over with."

"Please *don't* turn the lights on!"

"Must you do *that?*"

"Don't be such an animal!"

"You're absolutely *perverted!*"

A majority of men feel that their wives put the children first, that they themselves are nothing more than a meal ticket. Some wives let themselves go physically or intellectually, lose all interest in sex, or can't talk about anything besides the children, relatives, the neighbors, the bills.

At the other extreme, we have the man who married a woman so damned perfect and talented that she has taken control of the family finances, her husband and the children, and runs them all like a Marine Corps Sergeant. Her children and her husband, overshadowed by her domineering ways, become disheartened—admiring yet hating this "Superwoman"; they live in her shadow, emasculated by her forcefulness. This wife stayed with it—but is not in the least appreciated.

From boredom or discouragement, these married men seek Playmates. They want to escape the nitty-gritty: the piled-up bills, the hundred and one home repairs waiting to be done, the flat tire on Bobby's bike, the garage that needs cleaning—*again!* They are overwhelmed by *so* much to do and so little time to do it in. And then there are the kids—trying to discipline them fairly; trying to keep the family car going just one more year; trying to please their bored wife who is sick to death of being cooped up. Having hacked the business world all day, these men often want to stay home at night, and the two are at odds again: *she's* been home all week, and wants .to go out! An argument ensues, with the usual result—he slams out of the house and heads for the nearest bar to try his damndest to forget the whole thing.

All men want the sensuous female animal they have read about in bookstores, furtively hanging over the sex books. (Their wives wouldn't permit such smut in the house!) Bored married men know this female animal *must* exist; the sex books say she's real, but she's not waiting at home—at least not at their home! Then where is she?

And so the search begins. For some, "the search" is the whole objective. They see themselves in the mirror: the crease lines, balding temples, expanded waist line, flabby muscles. If they score with an attractive woman, they feel ten feet tall. And being menopausal and insecure, they will go on trying to score; that's their need.

Some men seek *only* a responsive sex partner; others are searching for someone to communicate with as well. Still others want a friend, a woman who thinks they are unique and special.

A man who is holding down a responsible management or decision-making position where one mistake

122

could cost him or his company hundreds of thousands of dollars, tends to exhaust his reserves of mental and physical stamina. This constant pressure brings on hypertension, nervous strain, ulcers, psychosomatic ailments, impotence. Very few escape with no side effects. Under such stress, a man seeks release from strain, and if his home life is not conducive to "unwinding," he may resort to alcohol, drugs, or a warm, comforting woman who will give him her undivided attention, yet be uninvolved in his business or personal life. She has no strings on him, and he is secure in the knowledge that he can walk away from her, any old time. She's an oasis in his highly motivated life, and can mean a great deal to him if she plays "The Game" according to the rules. If she pressures him, she will lose him; pressure is what he is running from.

On the other hand, the man who is frustrated in his career, who is facing forty and has evaluated his life and *knows* he has fallen far short of his goals, will also turn for comfort to a woman who is soft, feminine and understanding, who values him for qualities completely overlooked by his wife. By hanging on his words, building his scarred and disillusioned ego, she can make him feel like a real man again. She praises him, instead of making disparaging remarks. This woman is a priceless jewel; she can rejuvenate him, give him hope, show him that he is not a "zero."

Men and women have the same basic needs: physical, emotional, intellectual. If any of these needs are left unsatisfied in a marriage, a man will look around for a female Playmate to fill the gap. Men play "The Game" for the same reasons as women. After years of research, practical experience, and in-depth conversations with men of all ages and from every walk of life, I have compiled a list of the attributes men most hope to find in a female Playmate:

The primary demand is just what you would expect:

A warm and exciting sex partner, a woman who will actively respond in bed and enjoy every minute of it. This means kissing, feeling, touching—and innovating, taking the first step for a change, making the first move. Who wants to make love to a woman who just lies there like a sack of potatoes? A man wants an undulating, giving, anything-goes woman who appreciates and enjoys sex as much as he does, who doesn't act as though she is bestowing a priceless gift on a mere peasant because she allows him to enter her "inner sanctum." My advice to all females, especially wives, is: *get your ass in gear!* Don't just lie there: *respond!* The physical thrusts and movements unique to sexual intercourse *do* come naturally, so let yourself go, enjoy it, and your body will automatically do all the right things.

Oral-genital sex is another requirement. Most wives (the majority of married women I know have admitted this to me) feel that this type of sex is a *nasty, abnormal, perverted, degrading* act that only prostitutes, homosexuals, and sex perverts engage in. To these women I say: don't knock it 'til you've tried it!

Men love fellatio, or in slang terms, "blow jobs"— to have you use your mouth as a substitute vagina. As a form of love play, this variation is a tremendous ego-builder. A man is thrilled that a woman wants to please him *so* much. Mastering the technique will come naturally as you accumulate experience—the first time is the hardest.

Some wives will listlessly take their husband's penis into their mouth and lightly kiss it, and that's it! No motion, and motion is where it's at! And here's a helpful hint: after making love once, if you want your Playmate to achieve another erection, take it in your mouth. Instant resurrection guaranteed!

And picture this: you are engaged in oral-genital sex and, instead of mere love play, he ejaculates in your mouth! *Now what?* Swallow it. Period! If you can eat dead animals and fish, what's a little seminal fluid? Incidentally, seminal fluid contains, in addition to sperm, simple sugar, protein, citric acid (vitamin C), and enzymes, among other things. And, of course, there's no need for birth control.

Let's suppose he wants to do *"that"* to you! By *"that"* I mean cunnilingus, commonly called "eating out." (He uses his mouth and his tongue in place of his penis to stimulate your clitoris and vagina.) Does the idea turn you off? *"Try* it, you'll *like* it!" With his head in your genital area, tighten your legs around his neck and stroke his hair. Relax! Enjoy! Men love to taste you, and you'll learn to love it, too!

Nothing ventured, nothing gained. I used to wonder how anyone in their right mind could possibly eat frogs' legs . . . until one evening I gingerly tasted them for myself; now I can appreciate them for the delicacy they are. Remember, don't prejudge.

True, cleanliness is of vital importance, but bear in mind that doctors inform us that the mouth has more bacteria than the vagina and penis! Most women feel more comfortable about engaging in oral-genital sex if they have douched before leaving the house. Douching makes them feel cleaner and more desirable. Although the vagina is self-cleansing, some doctors recommend douching after menstruation. Theories vary, so check with your own doctor about this. Douching *too* often can cause serious problems; it makes you more prone to vaginal infections because it throws off the natural balance of bacteria normally found in the vagina.

Any form of love play is considered natural and normal, if both partners feel no inhibition. Some men dig being "jerked off" (using your hand to manipulate the penis until orgasm is reached). Usually, they want to masturbate you at the same time, inserting their finger into your vagina while stroking your clitoris. This type of "substitute sex" has its place, but it's only a substitute. You are probably dealing with a latent homo-sexual or a bi-sexual if *all* he wants is this type of action.

But remember, every sexual relationship is unique. Since your aim is mutual pleasure, oral-genital sex is not for everybody every time—it should happen spontaneously out of a deep feeling for each other.

Men love to have you fondle their penis. Try it when you and your Playmate have made love once and "the spirit is willing but the flesh is weak."

If you have any hang-ups about having sexual intercourse while menstruating, try inserting a diaphragm—it will contain the flow temporarily. Sexual intercourse during menstruation can help alleviate menstrual cramps and tension, and you don't have to worry about birth control. I have been told by Playmates that the vagina feels hotter during menstruation, although it is slicker than usual. So do whatever turns you both on; don't let menstruation interfere.

If, for some reason, you find your Playmate is having difficulty achieving orgasm, try this: pant, moan, groan, toss and turn, lift him up off the bed, go into a passion-ate frenzy, real or not! He'll flip *and* come.

And turn *on* the lights for a change! Who says it *has* to be dark to make love? There's no room for false modesty in this game. Don't be ashamed of your own body. Men love to look at a naked female. If your partner wants to make love with the lights on, *do it!* You *don't* have to be flawlessly built. Remember: "Beauty is in the eye of the beholder." Most women over thirty have some physical imperfections: sagging breasts, stretch marks, etc. *So what!* Don't be reluctant to let him see you naked. The first few times you are together, you may feel a little self-conscious and you probably won't be cavorting around like a nymph in your birthday suit; I admit it takes time and confidence. Your Playmate more than likely has a spare tire, is a

126

teeny bit overweight, is getting flabby in places, or is slightly bald. Do his physical imperfections turn you off?

Even if he isn't Mr. America, *you* find him sexually attractive, and that's all that really counts. Rest assured that in spite of your small breasts or appendix scar or whatever it is you're self-conscious about, your Playmate finds you desirable. My ugly gall-bladder operation scar has been described as "cute," and one of my Playmates worshipped my stretch marks as the badge of a real woman, the nucleus of life. If you're still shy about being naked, try taking a shower or, better yet, a bubble bath together.

Don't be afraid to experiment with new and different positions. Ever made love while sitting in his lap facing him? Most men love trying new ways and positions because their wives only do it in the so-called "missionary" position, man-on-top, woman-underneath. Do you want to bring him to an orgasm fast? *You* take charge: get on top of him with your knees supporting you, and give it all you've got; penetration will be deep and he'll come mighty fast!

Want to try something wild? How about sexual intercourse or oral-genital sex in front of the mirror with the lights on! Getting into position can be a little tricky: standing, you have to turn sideways a bit and lift your leg for insertion, but it's guaranteed to turn you both on as you watch. Oral-genital sex in front of a mirror is usually one sided, with your Playmate receiving. He will flip out seeing you on your knees making love to him. He has dreamed of this, now he's got it for real—living pornography in full-color, with *him* as the star!

So don't be afraid to innovate. The only limit is your own imagination. Making love in the shade of an old apple tree can be quite an adventure! So can making it in the front seat of a car—with the right partner!

Anal intercourse is not as uncommon as one would think. *No*—it is definitely *not* limited to homosexuals!

127

Lots of "normal" men and women engage in it. Naturally it depends on the individual couple and their feelings on the subject.

If you're interested, here's how: use plenty of lubricant, preferably K-Y. (It's not as messy as Vaseline!) Lie on your side in front of him, let him insert his penis just a bit, and ease backwards onto him at your own speed. Keep your breathing relaxed, so as not to tense your rectal muscles. At this point he must lie fairly still. There should be no pain if penetration is gradual and gentle; then he can take over, start moving and come to orgasm. If you stay relaxed, you'll experience a new kind of pleasure, difficult to describe. A man enjoys it tremendously and so will you if you follow the method I've outlined, and don't have any physical problems, such as hemorrhoids. (And with anal sex, you can forget about birth control!)

CAUTION: Tenderness and gentleness are essential here just as they would be with a virgin, because technically you are if you've never had intercourse in this manner before.

Some men like you to insert your index finger into their anus. They also might want to do this to you.

If your Playmate is fast on the draw, here's a hint how to slow down ejaculation: lie still and firmly apply pressure to the scrotum (on the side nearest the anus). This will hold back the semen and allow you both to continue longer, until you, too, reach orgasm. It is usually very difficult for a man with a new, exciting woman to hold back, even when he ordinarily has excellent control. But if, after having intercourse with him on several different occasions, he still reaches orgasm before you're ready, take matters into your own hands and slow him down. Men often have hang-ups about satisfying a woman and if he comes too soon every time, he will begin to feel he has failed you.

If this is the first time you've made love together and he makes it fast, rest assured that within a matter of minutes (yes, I said *minutes*) he will be ready to try again, and this time he will have more control.

All men like to be praised, so tell him how much you like his eyes, or smile, or dimple, or fuzzy chest, or fantastic mind, or whatever it is that you like about him, but be *honest!* Praise his best features; every man has at least *one* outstanding quality. Praise him often; sincere flattery, especially in bed, will stimulate him, but *forget the poetry*. Don't get romantic and emotional. Men love to hear: "I want you"—"Fuck me!"—"Your prick drives me crazy"—"I love to have you in me"— "Fulfill me; make me a woman"—but they *don't* want to hear "I love you." Instead of whispering "I love you" as you lay in his arms, try murmuring, "I love your body."

Stay with him, intellectually. Remember, he probably has a ding-a-ling waiting for him at home. (Excuse me, wives, I said "probably.") Be able to converse on a variety of subjects, from politics to cars, but don't dominate the conversation. He wants the limelight. If you are smart, you will soon learn your Playmate's likes and dislikes, and begin to share his interests. If he is a "middle-of-the-road" music fan and you like acid rock, start listening to his kind. If he is a sports enthusiast and digs football, basketball, baseball, etc., and you don't—*listen!* You'll learn. Stay away from religion. Chances are, you will have very definite ideas on the subject, and so will he; any discussion could lead to useless, endless debate. Keep your opinions to yourself and concede that he has a right to his own. The male ego will want to try to make you see the light if you don't see things his way.

Just as important as being a good conversationalist is being a good listener. He wants your undivided attention. If he wants to tell you about his afternoon on the golf course, stroke by stroke, *listen*. He will love you for it. If you know nothing about golf, have him explain the game to you.

12

AFFAIRS

When you meet a Playmate who turns you wild with desire and has everything else besides, you are now ready to join the rest of us who play "The Game." However, his interest in playing may not equal yours! Finding your "dream man" doesn't guarantee that he's going to feel the same way about you, even if he *is* tempted. So what are you going to do now, rape him?

While taking evening summer courses, I became strongly attracted to my extremely magnetic English teacher, Professor E. I was one of his best students and since he often called on me in class to answer questions or read my compositions, I assumed the attraction was mutual. He used to review our papers with each of us, individually, in his office. With every conference, as he sat by my side reviewing my papers, my attraction became stronger. I was sure it was mutual, but possibly because he was a professor and I a student, he never allowed a sexual relationship to develop. For our last conferences, he met me in the college cafeteria so that we wouldn't be alone. I was willing; he wasn't!

But don't despair. Although it may take a month or two before you finally encounter a man that you want and who wants you, don't give up. You *will* find him, sooner or later. And from then on, you're on your own. The best I can do is fill you in on what to expect.

First, we have the "One-Night Stand"—need I say more? This kind of encounter can't possibly be considered an "affair," but nevertheless, it happens all the time. It's sex-for-sex-sake, with *no* emotional involvement whatever. How can you become emotionally involved with a man you've only known for a few hours? Physical attraction is the key, and here is how it usually works:

A woman goes into a cocktail lounge feeling depressed, frustrated, lonely, or angry, has a quiet drink alone, meets a tall, dark and handsome stranger who turns her on, an hour later has sexual intercourse with him, returns home, and never sees him again.

This type of casual meeting is often used as a safety valve—a woman who has just discovered that her husband has been playing "The Game" often jumps into a "One-Night Stand" to get even; or, on the rebound from a deep but one-sided affair, she uses the "O-N-S" to rebuild her confidence. It does fill a need. At least for some women, sometimes. But this type of playing can be very dangerous—if you come out of it with a venereal disease, for instance. Suppose you don't even know the guy's name or where he works or how to reach him? At least if you're having a long-term affair, you'll know where it came from and both of you can get the necessary medical attention, with your Playmate picking up the tab, naturally. If you do try a "One-Night Stand," be careful!

Okay, I admit it—I succumbed to this type of fleeting relationship—once! It happened unexpectedly, as is usually the case. My husband was out of town on a five-day business trip and it happened that my annual gynecological check-up was scheduled to take place during his absence. My girlfriend, Lisa, went with me.

We had planned to have dinner afterwards, and go to the first class of a night course we were taking together.

My world came tumbling down that afternoon. The doctor discovered a lump in my breast and I was to go into the hospital Sunday, for surgery on Monday! His words, ". . . if the growth is malignant we will have to remove the whole breast," blew my mind! Numbly, I stumbled out of his office, and on the way to the restaurant broke the news to my girlfriend. Since I was too shaken up to eat, we ordered drinks. I was in a state of shock; the thought of losing a breast terrified me; and what if the growth was malignant and they didn't get it all, and the cancer spread throughout my whole body? I was scared to death!

Two men approached our table. One of them was a friend of Lisa's, so they sat down and joined us, ordering another round of drinks. Bob's relationship with Lisa was strictly platonic, but as his friend sat down beside me and introductions were made, I felt the blood rush to my face. Don was tall, blond, blue-eyed and had a fantastic body. He was thirty-two, divorced and had a great sense of humor—within five minutes he had us laughing like idiots. Needless to say, I kept my fears to myself. As far as the guys were concerned, we were just dining out to celebrate the start of the fall semester at school and the new courses we were taking.

Bob suggested dinner at his place. (He, too, was divorced.) We really weren't hungry, but we went along with his suggestion. Lisa sat beside Bob as he drove and I found myself in the back seat with Don. His hand had found mine—a hand I found comforting to hold. My fears were still there, but I no longer felt alone.

Bob's place turned out to be an old, restored New England farmhouse, complete with cows, horses, and ducks. The view was magnificent, and soon a cozy fire was blazing in the large fireplace, and we were all talking and munching on cheese and crackers and drinking wine while the steaks thawed.

Before I realized what was happening, I found my-self curled up on the couch in Don's strong, comforting arms. One thing led to another, and while Lisa and Bob were in the kitchen fixing dinner, Don led me upstairs to a bedroom. I didn't resist. Within minutes we were undressed and making wild, abandoned love! Afterwards, satisfied and feeling like a new woman, we ate a marvelous supper, and then they drove Lisa and me to our class.

Don called me a few days later and during the con-versation I learned what his "occupation" was. He was a "gigolo" (see Chapter Ten—"Playmates"). That was the end of *that* affair! He was currently living with an older woman! (Luckily, that lump on my breast turned out to be benign.)

Another time, a balmy summer evening after a night-school class, a girlfriend and I had stopped in at a local restaurant for a quick snack, when we ran into our mutual friend, Pat. Since the place was deserted and the night was still young, we decided to move on to a more lively spot. Off we went, the three of us, to a swinging lounge where we could drink and dance. Imagine: *two* attractive gals with one guy! I'm sure the men in the lounge couldn't figure out what was going on.

We had sat down and ordered, when along came a venturesome soul named Mark. Without a thought, I accepted his invitation to dance, leaving my two friends to their own devices. After several dances and the usual "What's your name? Where are you from?" etc., I learned that Mark was from St. Louis, divorced (he said), a field engineer for a well-known firm, and forty-four years old. Of average height, he was fairly attrac-tive, with black hair, beautiful blue eyes, but a bit of a pot; all in all, a nice guy. He joined us and the four of us had a marvelous time. Mark invited us up to his motel room for a nightcap and we accepted—my two friends were my protection.

Over drinks in Mark's room, we made plans to meet the following evening. He was in town on business, so it was "now or never" for us because he was scheduled to leave Sunday afternoon and this was Friday night! So the four of us met again the next night (my girlfriend's husband was away on a fishing trip). We split into pairs almost immediately, with Pat and my girlfriend going in one direction and Mark and I in another. Because he was leaving the next day, there was a desperation in our meeting which may have helped to plunge us into what followed—I spent the whole night with him. How did I get away with it, you ask? Well, I called my husband and told him I wanted to get away and was staying overnight with Carol, a friend of mine in another town. I called her and she agreed to cover for me if my husband should call. My husband was understanding—my parents had just died a few weeks back, three weeks apart, and he knew I was still battling depression.

During those magic hours Mark and I found a wholeness together most people never know. Watching him fly out of my life the next afternoon was heartbreaking because of our special affinity, but any type of permanent affair between us was geographically impossible —or so I thought! We kept in touch by letter and by phone and a few months later company business brought him back to my section of the country.

He called, but tried to talk me out of joining him at a city two and a half hours away—he didn't want to get me into trouble at home. But I wanted to be with him, so I told my husband I was going to see my brother in a town several hundred miles away to try to settle a family squabble that arose after my parents' death, and would be gone a couple of days. When he agreed, I phoned my brother and told him I wanted to be alone for a few days. Would he cover for me if my husband called? After much hesitation, he said he would, but hoped I knew what I was doing.

I was then able to spend two days with Mark in complete luxury, in the best hotel in town, at his company's expense, naturally. While he was working during the day, I was sunning myself by the pool. Our nights were idyllic; but by this time, Mark had finally admitted to me that he, too, was married, and long-term family ties being hard to sever, it was hopeless. Mark is imprinted in my heart, although I shall very likely never see him again. (He is now tied to a desk, wife, and family in St. Louis.)

The Affair

Then we have "The Affair." This is the relationship usually preferred by both sexes because it offers a certain amount of security; it is the adult equivalent of "going steady." Your Playmate is someone you enjoy being with, feel comfortable with and can talk to, someone you relate to sexually and who really turns you on. There is always emotional involvement as "friends and lovers." An affair of this depth can and often does go on for years, and usually the parting of the ways, when it comes, is friendly; the only real danger is a gradually increasing emotional involvement leading to "The Clinker," but more on that later.

My first affair with Playmate Paul is a classic example of a relationship that worked out very well for *both* of us; we *both* came out ahead. Because his wife was frigid, his sexual needs were not being met at home. Of course, he made love to her, but something vital was missing, and that's where I fit into the picture; I met a need that his wife couldn't (at least at that time). In return, he filled a gap in my life and thanks to him, in many ways I became a different person. I have no regrets. We are friends now, and occasionally lovers, because I had the sense to face facts: "Half a loaf is better than none."

Once you've mastered the art of emotional control, any affair is manageable. During my career-girl years, I met a very handsome, debonair sales representative from a nationally-known company. He stopped by my place of employment several times a month, always with a "Hi, beautiful. How's it going today? How about a drink after work?" I kept putting him off for months with pert remarks.

We all have days when everything we touch goes wrong and after a week like that I don't need to tell you how good my salesman, Ed, looked when he walked through the door with his usual "Well, don't you look nice today!" This time *I* said: "How about a drink together after work?" Ed was just great to me. He wined and dined me, listened to my woes, and being a perpetual optimist, he cheered me up. This "drink after work" eventually led to an affair and we spent many very satisfying hours together, until he took a new job in another part of the state. Our relationship dwindled to occasional phone calls, and finally to a mutual break. We are still friends; I can call him on a blue day and just hearing his voice lifts my waning spirits. I have no regrets, only sweet memories of a very humane, decent guy. Because he cared, he gave me hope and made me grateful to be alive.

A few years ago when my husband was transferred from one state to another, I returned to my home town temporarily, while my husband found a place for us to live. A nearby Air Force Base was holding an "Open House" one Sunday, and I went just for something to do. As I was touring the various installations, the loud-speakers announced a "Sentry-Dog Exhibition." Curious, I followed the crowd. As the men put the dogs through their paces, one by one, I recognized an old high school beau of mine with his dog, Liza. He hadn't changed a bit, still a good-looking turn-on, so I edged up to the ropes and called out to him. He looked at me, and it seemed at first through me—then recognition dawned. We talked briefly; he now had a wife and three kids, but nevertheless we agreed to meet the following night in a quiet restaurant for a drink, for old times' sake. Soon we were lovers. In the interim, until I left to join my husband, Steve and I had a ball. It was a beautifully satisfying physical relationship that ended spontaneously and with no heartache. He left me emotionally intact and satisfied.

The Clinker

Okay, here it is: "The Clinker." You've met your dream man, and you fell, baby, all the way and hard! You are at the point now where you want *no one* else but him; living in the same house and sleeping with your husband has become hell on earth! You and your Playmate have gone through the whole bit from start to finish; starting out with the usual cocktails, dinner and dancing once a week, then twice a week, then stolen afternoons together, then weekends. You know each other inside and out, everything. There is nothing taboo between you, you've done everything in all the sex books, and you're even intellectually compatible. You are totally in love.

Now what?

A lot depends on your situations: will *your* husband and *his* wife agree to a divorce? Are there young children? Will he take them? What about his children, the children he'll be giving up but still supporting? Will his wife let him go without destroying him financially?

Do you think your relationship could sustain itself on a day-to-day basis? Most of all, do you love each other enough to sever bonds—homes, mates, children, family—and start over fresh?

I learned from sad experience that when I had reached the point where I was ready to do this, my Playmate backed off with a thousand and one excuses why we should stay married to our current partners, and *he was 100% correct!* He wanted to keep meeting me as before, but marriage was out of the question. In this situation, you must be strong enough emotionally to shrug and say, "It is better to have loved and lost than never to have loved at all." If you want to play "The Game" you *must* keep your emotions under control at all times. The *consequences* will be serious if you fail to do this!

All I can tell you is I couldn't handle it emotionally when I first began to play "The Game." I still had unrealistic concepts of love and adultery.

Several years ago, I met a surgeon from Iran, Dr. H, at a social club Halloween party. Dressed as a dance hall girl, I still remember what he said, ogling the slit in my skirt and my exposed leg.

"Madame, is that a real gun in your garter?"

"No, not really, doctor, but then you're not really the Ace of Spades either, are you?"

By American standards, he probably wasn't handsome. He was balding, heavy-set, thickening at the waist. His eyes and accent were his calling card. Judging from the line of women just dying to hear all about Iran, I'd say he had a stacked deck.

"Doctor, what is your country like?"

"Is Teheran very ancient or a combination of East and West?"

"Have you met the Shah and the Empress?"

The doctor was the center of attention of all the bored middle-class housewives. He answered all our questions, obviously loving it. He was a real extrovert, suave and charming. Socializing was important in getting himself established, for he was new to the area and had just finished his residency. He'd struggled a long time to be able to say, "I am a surgeon"— he was almost forty.

The following spring, when I took my son to the hospital emergency room for treatment after a baseball accident, a lump was discovered on his wrist. I knew that it should be checked immediately, but as the orthopedic surgeon was booked for weeks, I had no idea where to turn. Then I remembered Dr. H, and nervously rang his office. To my surprise, he answered the phone himself. I blurted out, "Doctor H, this is Mrs. X from the social club; do you remember me? My son was in the emergency room just examined for what I thought was a baseball injury, but they think it's a ganglion and that he'll need surgery. Could you possibly see him?"

"Of course, Madame; why don't you bring him to my office at three this afternoon?"

"Doctor, I can't thank you enough. We'll be there."

Shall I ever forget that initial examination? After it was over, we left Andrew in the examining room and sat down in H's private office.

"Andrew has a ganglion of the wrist. This is minor— eighty to ninety percent benign. You mustn't worry. I will arrange for hospitalization and be in touch with you soon."

I said, "Doctor, I know I'm being the typical overprotective mother, but I'm frightened. Are you sure these ganglions are mostly benign?" I said.

"I assure you, Madame, it will be as I've told you," he replied.

Sensing my nervousness and concern, he offered me a cigarette. I slipped it into my mouth; he reached across the desk to light it. Nonchalantly, I tried to inhale, and was seized with choking, coughing, sputtering—a non-smoker trying to play sophisticate.

I had to call Dr. H the next morning to see if my son could continue playing baseball until his operation. He assured me there was no problem, then said:

"Madame, may I have the pleasure of taking you to lunch today?"

I'm sitting at the kitchen table in an old bathrobe, bleary-eyed, sipping brackish coffee, facing another day of monotony. Could he? He's got to be kidding.

"Why, yes, doctor; that sounds fine. One-ish?" My voice is calm, anyway.

"Drop by the office about one," H says.

My hair is a rat's nest. Damn it, my last pair of pantyhose has sprung a run. This dress is too business-like; that skirt and sweater are too sexy. How about this—sort of sexy-businesslike. Clean the house, wash the dishes, sweep the floor. It's almost time. Start rattling those jars and tubes—get beautiful!

I swing into the parking lot. Attractive, well-dressed, dark glasses; I enter the building. Here goes, chin up, nonchalant.

Up the stairs, ah, the office door again. H doesn't have a nurse yet. As I walk in, I hear him on the phone in the inner office talking to the emergency room. I thumb through the magazines trying to look like a patient. He walks down the hall towards me in his white coat.

"Madame, I'm so happy to see you. I will be with you in just one moment."

H joins me in street clothes.

"I know a charming restaurant across town."

"Fine, doctor; that sounds marvelous."

We start off in his top-down Buick convertible with M.D. license plates. I'm thinking: "Will you stop pressing against the door, stupid; you'll fall out. Everyone is *not* looking, just because you feel the car is lit up

141

like a Christmas tree." We're whipping along the highway. We arrive at the restaurant. It's one of the best in the area, colonial and quaint. We sit near the fireplace and the waitress takes our order.

"Two martinis, please," he says. We look at the menu. It's so huge that I can't see H across it.

I'm nervous, I don't know what to order. Our martinis arrive. I take too big a sip. My throat is on fire. I reach for the glass of water.

H says, "Madame, what would you like? This is such a special occasion for me. I don't often get a chance to relax."

Coolly, I reply, "Why don't you order for me? I like being taken care of."

The doctor is accustomed to taking command. He rattles off two orders to the waitress—I don't even know what H ordered. I sip and stare.

"Madame, you are so beautiful, such white skin. A feast for the eyes."

I sit blushing as the martinis are replenished. We're served. What a beautiful lunch. But neither of us is eating.

Having picked at our food, we now sit toying with our coffee cups.

"Madame, I simply could not eat. I have no appetite with such a beautiful woman so near me."

"Oh, you're exaggerating." I'm thinking, "Don't stop; I love it."

I don't know how, but our chairs have pushed together. They weren't when we came in. We're holding hands; I feel his knee touch mine. I'm floating on the most beautiful cloud-nine ever!

"Let's go now," H says. We walk out in a trance. At the car, he envelops me in a fierce embrace. The sun is hot. Sweat trickles down my breasts. H swings the door open. I crawl across the smooth leather seat. I'm bombed out of my mind, at noon, no less. There's a motel next door to the restaurant—convenient, no? As the motel door is closed, I'm held in a steel vice. How in hell did I get into the bed? And who's that moaning? I sound like a cat in heat! He is undressing, folding his clothes neatly and precisely, just like in surgery. He turns to me; I'm drowning in those eyes. He bends down to me, sinks into me. Entering, easing, darting, plunging, then holding back till I'm moaning. I see the love act reflected in his eyes as they expand and contract. He consummates; I lift him, gripping hard; we're clammy with sweat. Orgasm . . . for an instant, I black out. This is sex with my Persian surgeon. Dr. H laughs, relaxed, says he'll have to take karate to handle me.

H is operating on my son. I sit smoking in the waiting room. It's something to do, even if I don't smoke. I walk down the hall. H comes towards me, still in surgical cap and gown.

"H, is he all right?"

"Of course, darling," he whispers, "the growth is benign; everything will be fine."

"H, do you have any other surgery scheduled today?"

"No, but I must change, you know."

"The parking lot; half an hour," I whisper.

My son is in the recovery room. I can't see him for a few hours, so I'm taking off for a tryst with his surgeon. Crazy, wonderful world.

Lunch again. Damn, I wish I could eat, for a change. He orders shrimp cocktail for both; I force it down, burying it in cocktail sauce. H says,

"You don't like the appetizer? Please let me order something else for you."

"No, H, thank you," I mumble. How can I explain that I hate to waste time on food when I'm with him. I can hardly taste anything anyway. I only want to spend every precious moment with him *alone*.

So our clandestine meetings continued. This time H is angry that he desires me so. I go into the bathroom, run a glass of tap water. The glass falls and breaks. I come out with my hand wrapped in a towel. H is stripped down to his shorts. His clothes are neatly folded as usual.

"How I want you."

"H, I've cut my hand."

He pushes me down on the bed without a glance at the cut. H doesn't flip over a little blood. Later I think, "The maid will think someone was murdered in here." H dresses quickly; he's ready to go; I want to cuddle and relax a few minutes. H orders me to get dressed; he's due at the hospital. I'm in a bitchy mood.

"Just leave your hundred dollars on the dresser."

"I never speak of you this way. Why do you say such things of yourself?"

I think, "Why do I? I don't know."

"You come with me; you leave with me. That is final," H thunders. "What if my patient dies, and I was not available because of you?"

All right. I dress like lightning. Something has changed; the deep silence on the way home is a warning that I do not heed.

I've become deeply involved, waiting by the phone, writing him notes, wanting more of his time. H tries to explain—his pressing, demanding schedule. I am too self-centered to understand, and feel rejected.

The final confrontation occurs in H's office. He's been tied up for weeks. I lose my temper. "All right, drop me, you bastard. Keep your Buick and your padded wallet. You're going to need them. This is America. We don't have harems and concubines here."

I slam out of his office, gun the car and screech out of the parking lot. It's over. The deep affair begun in love has ended with hate.

It takes every ounce of courage to get over him. I am turned inside out, wounded in body and soul. It's an uphill battle, facing the death of an affair of this intensity.

If I'd known then how to play "The Game," it would not have been such a disaster. I'd have pushed less, enjoyed what we had, demanded nothing. He and I would still be friends.

13

PERILS OF "THE GAME"

"Daddy," inquired little Michael, "do fairy tales always begin with 'Once upon a time?'"

"No," replied the father, "sometimes they begin with 'I'm going to play bingo with the girls tonight, honey.'"

The most serious consequence of playing "The Game" is undoubtedly the risk of being caught in the act. What will your husband do if he has positive proof that you've been unfaithful? Will he "forgive and forget" the way all good, loving wives are supposed to do? Ha! Chances are he'll leave you and drag you through a humiliating and degrading divorce suit. Perhaps he'll even try to obtain custody of the children. And even if he's "big enough" to forgive your infidelity, he'll make your life a living hell. He will magnanimously state that he has forgiven you, but he never will, and he'll never miss an opportunity to remind you of your transgression with sarcasm, bitterness, and cynicism. Husbands love to punish verbally, it seems. So, unless you are caught red-handed, never admit the truth, for your own sake as well as your husband's.

There are several possible ways you might get caught playing "The Game."

What if you're out with your Playmate dancing in some out-of-the-way cocktail lounge and you suddenly notice your husband's boss and his wife standing there, staring at you in disbelief? You know instinctively that they are going to make a beeline for your house to "set your husband straight" about the type of woman you are! If this situation arises, your only chance is to say that you were very depressed and this guy offered to take you out for a drink, so on the spur of the moment you walked out of the function you had left home to attend, and went with him for drinks instead. Whatever you do, get home as soon as possible after you have been spotted; if the people who saw you with your Playmate have not yet told your husband, don't say anything about it. Tell him you felt sick so you left the meeting, or movie, etc., and came home. It will be easier to deny that the woman they saw was you if they don't mention it to your husband immediately, and if you're a good actress you should be able to deny it and bluff your way out of it. After all, if you're "the perfect wife" at home, how could you be out with another man?

Collision Course

There is a slim chance that you and your Playmate might become involved in an automobile accident. If it is a major accident and you end up in the hospital, it would be difficult to find a satisfactory explanation for your presence in some strange man's car, and your husband would have to know where you had parked your car and why. This is a bad scene, almost as bad as being caught in bed. I feel it would be best to admit

147

that you had skipped the place you were supposed to be going, and had gone instead to a cocktail lounge for a drink, had met this man and left with him to drive to an out-of-town bar where you wouldn't be recognized. Tell your husband that your Playmate had offered you a job (typing at home, or baby-sitting for his dog, etc.). Insist that nothing happened. Fake your way out of it. Remember, you are innocent until proven guilty!

Beautiful Dreamer

Do you talk in your sleep? If you do, your husband is liable to get quite an earful if you are playing "The Game." What if you started disclosing in intimate detail *aloud in your sleep* all the fantastic things that had happened between you and your Playmate? Remember, never admit anything; tell your husband that you were dreaming. Because of the kind of dreams *he* has, he'll probably believe you!

Who's George?

If you close your eyes and dream of your Playmate while having sexual intercourse with your husband, it is conceivable that, in the heat of passion, you might inadvertently say: "Oh George!" (and your husband's name is Bob!) Want to see an instant deflation? Try calling your husband by another guy's name! If this happens, say you were dreaming—name a soap opera hero. Your husband won't know the difference.

True Confessions

Speaking of "talking," you could become involved with a Playmate who "confesses" his infidelity to his wife, and believe it or not, he might even tell her *your* name! This actually *did* happen to me—*once!* My Playmate Paul blew his cool and spilled everything. His purpose was *not* to alleviate his guilt over his affair with me; he only wanted to hurt and humiliate his wife. *All* men who confess are actually saying to their wives: "See what you made me do!" Such a confession usually forces a wife to take a good, hard look at herself; maybe she has "let herself go" physically and he is ashamed of her; perhaps he has outgrown her; possibly she has become too wrapped up with the children, excluding him; or she may have become totally indifferent to having sexual relations with him. There could be any number of reasons why a Playmate confesses, but there is no excuse for him to name you! When my Playmate confessed to his wife and named me, he did not even end his relationship with me! This proves that guilt played no part in his confessing.

Some wives who play "The Game" also have a tendency to confess to their husbands. And they don't confess out of guilt or shame either; the name of their game is *attention!* Sometimes they confess over and over until they force their husbands to stop taking them for granted and treating them like a piece of furniture. This is guaranteed to shake a husband up. The results are usually negative—he'll never trust you again.

Take my advice: *Don't Confess!*

If you do, you will live with a twenty-four-hour-a-day watchdog. "Home" will become prison. Nothing you say or do will be accepted as the truth. He will watch you like a hawk and you will *never* be trusted to go out alone again. You blew it; divorce may be the only solution now. You have destroyed his manly pride! Shame on you!

Another plight that spells disaster occurs if a Playmate falls deeply in love with you and loses his head. If you are madly in love with him, too, that's fine; but what if you aren't? If he is insane about you and loses his objectivity, he could make your home-life a nightmare by phoning you day and night. I will assume that you have done everything in your power to make him understand that you are *not* in love with him, will *not* marry him, and *don't* want to see him again, in no uncertain terms! (See Chapter Nine: "Rules of 'The Game'").

If a Playmate starts bugging you at home tell your husband that you have been receiving obscene phone calls and get an unlisted phone number.

If he comes over to the house some evening to "have it out with your husband," either to declare his undying love for you or to confess he has had an affair with you, you're in for big trouble! The party's *over!* After all, how would a complete stranger know about that birthmark on your buttocks if he hadn't seen it! You could have a nasty situation on your hands, so admit to your indiscretion, but say it only happened once and the guy has been bothering you ever since. Admit as little as possible, and *always play it down!*

Never admit the truth, because your husband doesn't really want to know, no matter what he says to the contrary. If you can give him a plausible explanation, you'll salvage his pride . . . and probably your marriage. Remember, what he *doesn't* know won't hurt him. If you follow the rules set forth in this book and play your role of "wife" to perfection, your husband will find it impossible to believe that you were unfaithful. It is very unlikely you will actually be caught in the act of making love, unless you are being followed by a jealous husband or wife, or a private detective. If this happens, you're sunk!

Venereal Disease

Another very serious complication is venereal disease. How could you ever bluff your way out of that! My advice is: if you suspect that you might have picked up VD, run, don't walk, to your friendly, *discreet* gynecologist! Tell him the whole truth (without mentioning any names) and rely on his professional integrity. One of my girlfriends, Jill, did contract gonorrhea once, and after the usual tests her doctor gave her twenty-four hours to get her Playmate to his office to be checked. If Jill had failed to follow her doctor's orders, he would have had to report her case to the Board of Health, and they would have done the necessary follow-up work. Jill immediately phoned her Playmate and he went willingly to her doctor. He was beginning to develop the symptoms of the disease and was as afraid as she had been! Proper medical treatment was prescribed for both, but as it happened, the source of the infection turned out to be the *Playmate's wife,* who had been playing some games on her own! Because Jill's husband didn't know that she was taking "The Pill," they used condoms when they had intercourse, so there was no way for him to have caught her infection. Jill told him that she had developed a vaginal infection and the doctor wanted to examine him because it was highly contagious!

WARNING: If you are actively playing "The Game," it is *imperative* that you have both vaginal smears and blood tests every six months to make sure you haven't picked up VD. Some types of venereal diseases have *no* symptoms at all, *until* the infection is well established. Remember, an ounce of prevention is worth a pound of cure!

Pregnancy

One of the more serious risks of playing "The Game" is impregnation by a Playmate. If you and your Playmate happen to get carried away some evening, throw caution to the wind and fail to use adequate birth control, you could find yourself pregnant with *his* child! If you suspect that you might be pregnant (wait until your menstrual period is at least a week overdue) get busy and seduce your husband, supposedly using no contraceptive. (Use your diaphragm if you have one, just don't let him know it's in.) Get him drunk, climb on top of him in the middle of the night, use any method short of actual rape to make love to him, so that later, if necessary, you can attribute your pregnancy to him: "Remember that night we got carried away and didn't use any protection?" Then, when your period is two weeks late, see your obstetrician. He alone can determine if you are pregnant or if your menstrual period has been delayed for some other reason. Worry can sometimes raise havoc with the menstrual cycle, and so can a guilty conscience.

If you *are* pregnant, *don't panic!* It's not the end of the world. Remember, the U.S. Supreme Court has barred the states from interfering with the decision of a woman and her doctor to terminate a pregnancy within the first three months; so in effect the abortion laws of all states have been ruled invalid. It may take a year before abortion is legalized in your state, and even when it is you will be faced with a few problems: would your husband go along with your decision to have an abortion? You'll have to use his health insurance to pay for it, you know, unless your Playmate is willing to foot the bill. If you decide to have an abortion without your husband's knowledge, you could probably get away with telling him that you had to have a D & C (dilation and curettage). Naturally, if your husband has had a vasectomy, your goose is cooked; your egg is laid! Abortion or divorce are your only solutions.

A couple of years ago, one of my friends, Lucy, had the misfortune of becoming pregnant by her Playmate, with whom she was deeply in love. After her obstetrician had confirmed her suspicions, she was faced with perhaps the most serious decision of her life: What should she do? At that time, only two states, New York and California, had legalized abortion, and making a trip to one of these states would require money and an air-tight excuse for her absence. Lucy decided to take the bull by the horns and she informed her husband of her pregnancy and of her desire to have an abortion out-of-state. But upon learning of her condition, her husband was overjoyed and refused even to consider letting her "get rid of" the unborn child, even though they already had several children. Lucy, too, had some reservations about having an abortion, on moral grounds. This left her with two choices: confess to her husband that she had been unfaithful and that the child she was carrying wasn't his, or have the child and let her husband think he had fathered it.

What would you have done?

Confessing the truth, she would have lost everything; so she said nothing and had the child. She made the best of a situation that could have been disastrous. Fatherhood is more than just a biological act; almost any man can "father" a child, but it takes a real man to be a father. The child has added a new dimension to her husband's life; shortly after the baby was born he contracted mumps, which left him sterile. To Lucy, the child is the personification of the love she felt for a truly fantastic man, and now part of him will be hers forever.

Disaster!

Although this is a million-to-one risk, let's discuss it anyway. What if some night, at an out-of-town motel, in the wild throes of passion, your Playmate has a heart attack or a stroke and dies? I'm serious—what would you do? Remember, your car is back in town—his is parked out in front!

Here's how I'd handle it: First, roll him over on his back and elevate his head and shoulders. Next, check his clothing for any medication he might be carrying. If you find any slip a pill under his tongue. Now get dressed *fast,* and call the motel manager and tell him you have an emergency on your hands. He should be there within seconds.

If before the ambulance and the police arrive, you know for certain that your Playmate is dead, leave as discreetly as you can, walk to the nearest bar or restaurant or drug store, and cool it until you've pulled yourself together. Then call a trusted girlfriend, tell her where you are and what happened, and have her pick you up and drive you back to where your car is parked.

If your Playmate is still alive, *stay with him* until the ambulance and police arrive and go to the hospital with him if necessary. You can always bluff your way out of this mess with the "good Samaritan" bit: tell your husband and the police that you met this guy in front of the place where you told your husband you were going and he was obviously ill, so you stopped and offered whatever aid you could render. Say that he wanted to go somewhere to lie down and rest and take his pills, that he assured you "his condition" was chronic and not serious, and so you drove him in his car to the motel and stayed with him while he rested. But naked? Oh well, you *could* have modestly gone into the bathroom while he stripped down!

Overcommitment

Another danger: Adultery can and will be disastrous if you let your emotions get out of hand. You can get very moody and irritable, neglect your home, children and husband, have difficulty concentrating on your job, start drinking or pill popping, start smoking too much, cut your husband off sexually, or take on any strange man as a substitute, as you wait by the silent phone. To play "The Game," you must have strength. You can fall into a severe depression if you are unexpectedly dropped by the big love of your life Playmate. The results can be devastating.

A close friend of mine, Tina, suffered a nervous breakdown when a Playmate of two years' standing disappeared without a word or a forwarding address. A few months after his departure, she did hear from him, but by then it was too late—the damage was done. She tried to adjust to it, but found herself out of it, not functioning. She withdrew, couldn't eat or sleep, stopped caring about her personal appearance, wanted to destroy the things she owned, and herself. She was hospitalized for depression, and after two weeks in a private hospital, was committed to a state mental institution for observation. Perhaps the shock of her surroundings and the knowledge that she had hit rock-bottom made her fight to gain her equilibrium. She was released after ten days and fought her way back to stability. She was one of the lucky ones!

Before you start playing "The Game" you must accept adultery for what it is.

A game.

An escape from boredom.

An alternative to divorce.

Draw the line emotionally and accept the situation for what it is, or you and innocent members of your family will be hurt. (If you end up in a mental hospital, what's going to happen to your family?)

Ninety-nine percent of the men who play "The Game" are definitely, positively *not* interested in a permanent commitment—marriage. They want you as a mistress, not a wife; they already have one of those, remember? If you get deeply involved with a Playmate, you are the one who will suffer if he grows tired of you and walks out of your life. If you feel yourself getting over-involved, get out fast. Break it off! Stop seeing him. Your sanity may be at stake—*literally!*

Find a new interest *fast.* Force yourself to try some of the games discussed in Chapter Three as stop-gaps to survive and overcome it: the secret is to get involved in something—*fast!* If it's spring, start a garden. Redecorate your home (at least one room anyway) or take up a hobby that fills your time. Work off your tension, if at all possible. Don't just sit there brooding about him. This will only weaken your willpower. Shut him out of your mind, keep busy, and I guarantee your suffering and pain will pass; it *will* ease. Time heals all wounds!

14

SURE SIGNS THAT YOUR HUSBAND'S PLAYING

Let's assume for the moment that it suddenly dawns on you that your husband has been putting in quite a bit of overtime lately, or that he's spending almost all of his free time working out at the health spa, or playing cards, or bowling, or attending more meetings than usual, etc. Is he *really* where he says he is and doing what he says he's doing? He *could* be playing "The Game." And if you have always been a faithful wife, you will be shocked and horrified and furious at his infidelity. And if your suspicions are confirmed, you will feel betrayed, degraded, and heartsick.

"How could he do such a thing?" you'll ask yourself. "Why?" "How have I failed him?" You will be plagued with self-recriminations—"If I had fulfilled his needs this never would have happened," you'll think. Well, you're wrong. Your husband probably loves you deeply, but for reasons discussed elsewhere he got involved because of some unfulfilled need. This does not mean that he no longer loves you or values you for what you are: a competent housewife, a great cook, a loving mother, etc. However, these qualities may not be enough to prevent him from playing "The Game"— at least once!

It's another story if you are playing "The Game"

yourself. Then, if you discover that your husband has something going himself, you will probably be more understanding; not that the knowledge is going to hurt any less, but after all, you know what playing "The Game" is all about and that it *is* a game. Therefore, you won't feel as threatened by it. Nevertheless, it's going to hurt your ego, unless you are made of stone.

If you suspect that your husband is playing "The Game," there will be many giveaway signs. Men, it seems, aren't as adept as women when it comes to playing "The Game" without detection.

How often he changes his underwear is a classic giveaway. Most men change (hopefully) once a day, so if you suspect that something is going on, count the number of "T" shirts and shorts in his bureau drawer. If you notice that he is changing his underwear before he goes out for the evening, beware! He may also suddenly decide that all his underwear is shabby or too small or too large for him, and use one of the above excuses to purchase several new, snowy-white sets, when up until now you have always taken care of buying them. You know how vain men are, and a man who is playing "The Game" doesn't want his Playmate to see him in old, gray, stretched-out underwear! It could destroy his image! If he is bold enough, he may even buy some of the new bikini briefs!

Speaking of clothes, he may suddenly decide to go "mod"—after you've been begging him for years to throw away his cuff-bottomed, pleated-front pants and out-of-style white shirts! Out of the blue, he may spend a small fortune on flared or bell-bottom knit pants, brightly colored shirts, flashy ties! And this guy, who has worn nothing but conservative black oxford shoes, buys himself a pair of ankle-high, zippered boots! Knit jackets, too! Why the sudden interest in clothes?

Another tip-off: he may decide to let his crew-cut grow out in favor of sideburns, and he may even visit a men's hair stylist. If he is bald, he may decide to be fitted for a toupee! Perhaps he'll grow a beard and a mustache! Some men even decide to dye their hair to cover the gray!

Another clue can be found in the number of baths or showers he takes and how often he changes his clothes. For some men, it's completely normal for them to shave, shower and change clothes before leaving the house for the evening to attend a meeting or a sports event, or to visit a client or play cards, etc. If this has been an established pattern for the past fifteen years, don't worry about it. But if he suddenly becomes a bathroom fanatic, showering and changing his clothes almost every time he leaves the house, even when he is supposedly going over to so-and-so's house to help him paint a ceiling, be prepared to accept the fact that he might be playing "The Game."

How often he shaves is another sign. Some men shave just once a day; others twice a day. If he changes his normal shaving pattern, whatever it is, this could be a tip-off. Men who are playing "The Game" live in fear of giving their Playmate a beard rash. Does he shave before he makes love to *you?* I doubt it!

Another giveaway: he may become the Avon Lady's best customer, purchasing all kinds of beauty aids for men—after-shave lotions, hand and body creams, men's hair spray, etc. Now you can smell him before you can see him!

It takes money for a man to play "The Game"; money for dinners, drinks, motels, etc., so you may notice a change in your finances. Money may become scarce, unless he is on an expense account and can write off his Playmate as a business expense. If up to this point he's always turned his paycheck over to you and you've been writing the checks and paying the bills, he may decide that *he* wants to manage the budget! Or if he normally pays the bills and gives you a weekly sum for household expenses and groceries, he may cut it. If you suspect that he is playing "The Game," check the monthly bank statements; look for cancelled checks made out to "CASH" and see who endorsed them—a motel, maybe?

Another crystal-clear giveaway: he may become irritable, arguing with you over senseless, stupid things. This is a classic "cover" men often use for an excuse to get out of the house at night. Generally speaking, it is a lot easier for a man to get out at night than it is for a woman, but when he *has* to get away for the evening and has no excuse, he will often resort to a senseless argument; then he can blow his stack and walk out, in a rage!

Okay, here's how to beat him at his own game: don't argue with him—agree. If he rants and raves because the kids' toys are scattered all over the living room (as usual), apologize and pick them up. If he decides he hates what you've cooked for dinner, which up until now has been his favorite dish, offer to cook him whatever else he'd like. In other words, take the wind out of his sails by agreeing with him, keeping your cool; remember, it takes two to argue. He'll have to come up with another reason for getting out of the house and he will be frantic, especially if he has a meeting with his Playmate arranged for 8:30 PM! Don't get me wrong; he *will* find an excuse to leave the house, even if it's just to run to the store for a pack of cigarettes. Naturally he won't come home for several hours even though the store is only a block away, and when he does he'll have some flimsy excuse: "I met Bill and we decided to stop for a couple of beers"—and by now it's 1:00 AM!

You will probably notice a definite mood change. He may be edgy, moody, withdrawn, tense. After all, it's not easy for a man to lead a double life. His drinking at home may increase. Instead of his usual drink before dinner, he may now start drinking continuously until bedtime. His smoking may also increase.

Or the exact reverse could happen: he may go out of his way to be a "model" husband, cleaning out the messy cellar or garage voluntarily—a job you've been after him to tackle for months! He may wine and dine you, buy you flowers and gifts, give you money for new curtains, etc. Any sudden change like this could indicate that he has some action going on the side and feels guilty about it.

Here's another symptom: some men who are playing "The Game" lose all interest in sex at home. You could be wearing the sexiest, briefest nightie and look your most desirable, but he's "too tired" or "has a headache"! Now *that's* a switch! Or you may unexpectedly find yourself living with a sex maniac! The guy who usually only wants to make love two or three times a week *now* wants to have intercourse two or three times a *day!* This *can* happen, and if it does it usually means that he is strongly physically attracted to someone else, but hasn't consummated the affair. In fact, he may be trying his darndest to stay straight despite his strong physical attraction for someone else. So keep him happy, sexually.

Generally, if your husband is playing "The Game," some or all of the above changes in behavior will occur. Now, how do you determine if he really *is* playing "The Game"? Some of the ways I've already mentioned. Here are a few others: you could discreetly check the ash tray in the car for lipstick-stained cigarette stubs, and the seats and floor for bobby-pins, earrings, etc., although I doubt that you'll find anything. He's probably not *that* dumb! Check his wallet while he showers, and his bureau drawers—you just might come across something; perhaps a woman's name and phone number, a motel receipt, etc.

Try this: some night when he is supposedly going to

a meeting ten minutes' drive away, dash out to the car while he's busy in the bathroom, and record the mileage on the odometer. In the morning as he's leaving for work, run out to the car, give him a letter you want to have mailed or a clean handkerchief, memorize the last three numbers on the odometer and compare them with the number you wrote down the night before. If the figures show he's driven fifty miles, you *know* it wasn't any ordinary meeting. He had a more interesting place to go.

You could always come up with some emergency at home that demands his attention—replacing a good fuse with a burned-out one—instant crisis, and an excuse to call him! Call him at the place he's supposed to be. Chances are he won't be there, but if he is you can tell him about the "emergency" at home and he'll never suspect that you were really just checking his alibi!

Fine. All the pieces fit. You are convinced beyond a shadow of a doubt that your husband is playing "The Game."

Now what are you going to *do* about it?
THINK BEFORE YOU ACT.

Your whole future could be at stake. If you confront him with your suspicions he will probably deny them. But what if he doesn't? What if he admits that he's involved with another woman? Then what?

Let's be practical. Do you have children? Is he a decent, hard-working guy and a good father and husband? We will assume that the answers to the above questions are "yes" and that this is the first time he has been unfaithful. FACT: "Fifty percent of married males and twenty-six percent of married females have experienced extramarital copulation by the age of forty."*

---

* *The Naked Ape*, Desmond Morris. Chapter II, page 76.

If I were *you,* I'd stay cool, say nothing and play "super-wife." By "super-wife" I mean that when he goes out after dinner "on business," you kiss him goodbye with a smile and tell him that you hope the meeting goes well. If he calls from the office to tell you that he has to work late and not to wait up for him, say "That's all right, dear, I understand." And before you go to bed, fix him a snack and leave the light on in the kitchen with a note saying that you knew he'd be hungry when he got home, and have fixed him a little something so he wouldn't go to bed on an empty stomach.

Get the idea? Yes, it's going to be difficult, but in the long run it will pay off. Go out of your way to be nice to him and he'll feel guilty as hell. If you love him and want to stay married, give him a chance to get the affair out of his system.

And for God's sake, *forget* all that garbage you've read in the women's magazines about winning him back by seducing him in a sexy nightgown. After all, he is probably having sexual intercourse with a new and attractive woman, and until the novelty of it wears off, face facts: he's made love to you for years, and the other gal turns him on more than you can, at this point. You're old hat to him, so don't try the sex angle; it could do more harm than good! *Bide your time.* Sooner or later the affair will end and he will feel guilty and ashamed, if you have been playing "super-wife."

WARNING: Some evening, after his affair is over and he has settled down, he may turn to you and say: "Honey, there is something I have to tell you." This is a tip-off that he is ready to play "True Confessions," something that you should *not* let him do! Remember, what you *don't* know can't hurt you! In this case, ignorance is bliss! It is difficult enough knowing that he has been unfaithful, even though he doesn't know you know, but if you listen to his "confession," you could end up destroyed. You will *never* be able to forget it if you hear every intimate detail! No matter how curious you are, nip his "confession" in the bud. Admit to him that you know he has had an affair, but tell him that you honestly don't want to hear about it. He will be shocked himself when you tell him that you knew about the affair. He thought he was playing it super-cool and had you snowed! Suggest that he seek professional help, a psychiatrist, maybe, who can help him cope with his guilt and offer concrete suggestions. Reassure him that you will willingly see a marriage counselor, if he thinks this will help the situation.

Let's suppose that you're not the type to cool it once you have proof or suspect that he's playing "The Game." Then you will probably confront him with your suspicions and proof, if you have any. The results of this confrontation *could* be disastrous, to say the least! Who knows, he may walk out; don't forget, *you* have forced the issue.

Good for you, you had enough "pride" to throw the infidel out! Where will this move leave you? What about the mortgage payments? And food? And other household expenses? Can you go to work and earn enough to meet the monthly bills and pay a baby-sitter if necessary, or will you be forced to apply for welfare? You may lose the house and end up living in some dingy apartment. How are your children going to take this new change in life-style? Is your pride that important? Why not forgive and forget? Give him a second chance! What have you got to lose?

15

DEVELOP YOUR POTENTIAL

Take a critical look at yourself in a full-length mirror. What do you see? An overweight, skinny, frumpy, dowdy, messy-haired housewife wearing her husband's old shirt, a faded pair of blue jeans, no make-up? You think: "How can this over-the-hill has-been be what men consider a turn-on?" You think it's just impossible? I say you're wrong!

Any woman can be attractive without spending a fortune. Buy, or borrow, a copy of *The Sensuous Woman,* by "J." This candid book will show you step-by-step, in vivid detail, how to become a truly desirable woman. "J's" easy instructions are a must for any woman who wants to develop her potential. Even if you never play "The Game," you owe it to yourself and to the man in your life to make the most of yourself. Free your imagination; use it constructively. Dependence will lessen as you become more confident.

There's no point in kidding yourself. If you want to score, shape up! Beauty isn't the prime requisite. Making the most of your outstanding features, concealing your weak points, revitalizing your mind, keeping your health up to par, acquiring confidence and poise; these are the imperatives. Remember, it's not what you plan, it's what you do with yourself that counts!

There aren't many women with the face and figure of a Raquel Welch. How attractive you are isn't just the luck of genetics—classic features, naturally curly hair, etc. The basis of an outstanding woman is physical and emotional fitness, a receptive mind, good posture, good grooming, normal weight, a shining, attractive hair-do, clever make-up, and self-confidence.

Take stock of yourself, objectively. Don't be discouraged by imperfections; a weight problem, breasts that seem too large or too small, irregular features, heavy hips, too tall, too short, a badly proportioned figure, gray hair, glasses, bad skin, excess facial hair, etc., are all obstacles that can be overcome. Appropriate clothes, exercise, adequate rest, proper skin care, make-up tricks, attractive glasses or contact lenses, electrolysis, proper hair care, wigs, diet, can solve most of what you consider terrible problems. Believe me, they're not. Keep in mind that beauty is in the eyes of the beholder and in the hands of the creator. All these problems can be solved once you make up your mind to do something.

Your Hair

For years, you have probably been "styling" and cutting your own hair, recklessly chopping at it whenever your reflection in the mirror unnerves you. Maiming your hair is a very poor way to economize. A professional hair cut in a style you can easily maintain at home is essential. Choose a salon with a good reputation. If you're dissatisfied, switch. Ask the attractive women you know who cuts their hair.

If your hair is graying or just dull and drab, a trip to your drugstore or dime store will remedy the problem. A simple-to-use hair color kit (either permanent or vegetable dye), or one of the new foam-ins, can remedy your problem in a half-hour. If you're wise, you'll choose a shade close to your original color. If you want to try a dramatic change, try frosting or a total stripping, if your hair is almost white. Be careful of brassy blond or red or deep black shades; they harden and age the face. If you want to experiment, try a wig. They're very reasonable and a lot easier to remove than permanent hair dye.

Buy a couple of hair pieces, braids, curls, wiglets that match your hair color. You can then have an easy-care basic style, that can be changed in minutes to a glamorous or more formal style.

A warning on permanent hair dyes. The bleach tends to dry your hair and cause split ends. And don't let home hairdryers and electric rollers get too hot—they cause the same problems. Use protein shampoos and conditioners and protein setting lotions. If you have none on hand, massage a dab of mayonnaise through your hair and leave it on about fifteen minutes before shampooing. Use shampoo especially made for tinted hair and rinse it with dark vinegar. Shampoo a day before your hair shows it needs it. Occasionally brush your hair with baby oil to moisturize and stimulate the scalp. Remember hair sprays and lacquers are drying; counteract this with conditioners. If your hair is limp, there are several products on the market that add body. An old stand-by is to rinse your hair in beer after shampooing. Don't knock it till you've tried it.

Your Skin and Make-Up

If you are thirty or over, a moisturizing of your face, neck and body is essential. Apply hormone cream (follow the directions carefully) to your face and throat, massaging it in with upward strokes. Use eye cream to fight crow's-feet around the eyes. Cleanse your face thoroughly every night. Steam, then rinse with a solution made with boric acid (one teaspoon to a pint of water). Pay special attention to blemish areas; a medication containing sulfur will help heal. Try hypo-allergenic make-up if you have an ultra-sensitive skin, or use medicated make-up.

Choose creams carefully according to your skin type: normal, oily or dry. Too much cold cream will aggravate an oily skin; too much astringent will irritate a dry skin. Every morning, apply a light moisturizer under your make-up. When at home, wear no make-up. Let your skin breathe. Use a lip gloss or Vaseline to ease cracking or drying lips.

To lighten a ruddy complexion, use a slightly greenish-tinted under make-up toner before applying make-up. To liven up a very pale complexion, dab extra make-up under the eyes and apply a little blusher to the cheek area. For shiny looks, coat the face with a bit of baby oil. If you want a velvet look, use make-up, then powder and blot dry. Then make-up again.

Don't neglect the rest of your body. Adding oil to your bath lubricates your skin; a handful of baking soda will remove perspiration, excess oil and impurities. Use moisturizer on elbows, legs, feet—all over. Use a pumice stone to keep your heels smooth. Never say, "I don't have time." If I have time, so do you—no excuse. To cover varicose veins, use a leg make-up or dark stockings. If the veins protrude, see a doctor—they can be removed. If you follow all of the above and some of the tips you already know, you will soon hear "how young she looks," and who doesn't want to hear those sweet words? Get in the habit of freeing your face of tension lines—they can become permanent. Try not to scowl so much.

Keep your make-up light during the day; you can go to heavier and more dramatic make-up at night. Keep your brows well plucked, and pencil them lightly. Try using two flattering shades of eyebrow pencil such as medium and dark brown; then dab lightly with baby oil or Vaseline. At night, use a deeper eyeshadow than you do by day; try silver and iridescents for a dramatic effect. If you wear glasses, remember to accentuate your eyes. Try eyeliner, mascara and artificial lashes.

Remember, a heavily made-up woman looks older not younger. The object is to use make-up for a young, natural look. Keep it subtle—avoid deep red or purplish lipsticks, regardless of the current fashion fads.

Use an oily remover for eye make-up to lubricate your lashes and prevent drying and irritation of the delicate skin around the eyes. If you wear mascara, give those lashes some TLC. There's a new special brush-on protein treatment that moisturizes lashes and keeps them beautiful.

Do you have excess hair in the wrong places? Electrolysis is a permanent answer. Shaving, bleaching, waxes and cream depilatories are all effective but temporary. And shaving does not make the hair coarsen —that's a myth.

Do you have freckles? They are intensified by exposure to sun and wind. Use an ointment that shields against ultra-violet rays, or cover them with make-up. Be careful of skin bleaching creams containing mercury. Too much can be dangerous or cause a skin rash. Or how about just enjoying them. Doris Day doesn't let freckles faze *her*.

Do you suffer from bad breath? Brush your teeth regularly; use dental floss and a chlorophyll mouthwash.

Do you have unsightly nails? Try protein gelatin capsules or a proteinized nail polish. Don't use bright or dark nail polish; use clear or natural polish until your nails improve. Give them an oil treatment now and then; polish remover tends to be drying. Keep fingernails and toenails manicured. Never leave the house with chipped polish; remove it quickly and apply a base coat till you have time for a good manicure.

Do you wear glasses? Try to have at least two styles

plus a pair of prescription sun glasses. Glasses are now a fashion accessory, available in dozens of attractive, flattering styles. Or you might try contact lenses.

Choose a perfume that you feel represents you and make it your trademark. Splash it all over your body; wear it twenty-four hours a day and love it.

Listen to yourself on a tape recorder. Do you like what you hear? If your voice sounds grating, whining, or nasal, try to moderate the tone, pitch it lower. Make a habit of hearing yourself speak.

Do you have a weight problem? Join Weight Watchers or a weight-control group, or see a doctor. Buy a dress two sizes smaller, and make up your mind that it will fit you very soon. If you're too thin, make an appointment with your doctor for a check-up.

Don't settle for just getting by. Look in the mirror; that run in your stocking is going to get worse. Stop it with a drop of nail polish. You're going to lose that button—sew it back on. Those scuffed shoes need a quick brush or polish. That scroungy purse ruins your look. Those dirty gloves—change them for fresh ones. That sagging hem—mend it. Take stock again. Exit left. You're beautiful.

Your Clothes, Posture, Attitude

First and foremost, your posture: stand straight. An expensive gown will look frumpy if you're slumped over. If you are tall, wear low shoes—but don't slump. Pull in that stomach, straighten those shoulders. How you stand and walk affects your shoulders, bust curve, stomach curve—your overall presentation. That's Lesson One and don't forget it. Walk with grace. When you sit, bend at the knee and slide into your seat; don't go down low end first. Bend straight down to pick up something, not over. Sitting down, cross your legs.

I know many of us are on limited budgets. Sew your own clothes, salvage and remake some of your old outfits. Try to stay with the latest fashion trend, but only if it is right for you. The mirror will give you your answer. Accessorize and coordinate outfits with a scarf at the waist or in your hair, jewelry, attractive handbags, shoes, gloves. Wear beads, leather necklaces, anything unusual. Keep a sharp watch on sales and discounts on good clothing in good stores. If I can do it so can you. At a dinner dance, I heard a woman say, "She must have a closet the size of a ballroom!" I don't even have a closet in my room, and in fact my room is the size of a closet.

Your Health

Health is a state of complete physical, mental and social well-being and not merely the absence of disease or infirmity.

World Health Organization
1946

Never underestimate the importance of your health. You can develop a full potential; but you'll not get far without the above. It is the first and most important asset.

To keep your physical health up to par, you must have adequate sleep. If you have insomnia, try a warm milk-and-honey nightcap. A well-balanced diet is essential. If you suspect yours may be deficient, use a vitamin supplement. Iron tablets during your menstrual period may prove helpful, too.

Exercise regularly but moderately. A brisk walk every day can't be equalled. For tension, try saunas, yoga, health clubs. Keep yourself in shape with a dance or gymnastics class—exercise should be fun too. Get a complete physical and pelvic exam at least once a year. Don't be a hypochondriac, but if disease symptoms persist, see a doctor. If you are overweight, you're probably eating too much and exercising too little. If you must diet, sufficient sleep is important.

Your Intellect

Start by sweeping away those cobwebs in your brain. Does your conversation center around which soap is best for your laundry, how to potty-train Junior and why the dye ran from your new bedspread? This may be interesting to other women, but don't expect a guy to be fascinated by it. It's a big world out there. Start finding out more.

Begin by reading the newspaper, all of it, including the news, editorials, business and financial sections. Read at least one book a week, and not just cookbooks or *True Love* stories. Vary your reading with best sellers, classics, nonfiction. Open up that good mind of yours. Try educational television, controversial talk shows, plays, current events, news. Read varied magazines, join study, philosophy groups. Let a little knowledge shine in. You'll be surprised how quickly you can contribute intelligently to any discussion instead of sitting there feeling like a reject from society. Improving your mind will build your self-confidence too, as you become more knowledgeable about many facets of life.

Your Sexual Potential

Are you still with me? Good. By now you're attractive, intelligent, and healthy. What about your sexual potential?

Practice makes perfect, gals. Now get with it! Begin by making advances to your husband. You heard me. Where else are you going to find a penis to experiment with? Practice is essential for acquiring bedroom technique; you've got to start somewhere to get rid of those puritanical ideas and inhibitions.

Some evening, while he's sitting half-asleep in front of the television set, put on your most provocative negligee, fix a couple of drinks, and come in half-naked and smiling. Your husband will think he's dreaming; pretend this is your fantasy "dream man" and move in.

Wives frequently complain:

"Having intercourse with my husband is dull and boring."

"I go through the motions."

"I wonder if I'm really frigid?"

Is this an accurate description of your feelings? Gals, I've got news for you; your vagina hasn't gone dead. When you go to your gynecologist for your annual pelvic examination and he inserts that speculum in your vagina, it feels cold and uncomfortable, doesn't it? This proves you do have sensations there, you're not damaged by child birth. If you're partially frigid, it's psychological; it's your mind that's turned off. In the arms of that handsome, sexy "dream man" of yours, you'd have no trouble feeling his penis in you and reaching a climax, would you?

Let's be frank. How often do you say, "Oh no, not now," to that love-starved husband of yours? If he approaches you more than once a week, do you consider him a sex maniac? Start thinking "yes," for his sake *and* your own. Train your body to respond. Before you know it, you'll be enjoying sex again.

Confidence comes from practice in everything we've been talking about. It's simple; you *are* what you *think* you are. Once you start believing in yourself, confidence comes naturally. I know—I've walked this road. As you rejoin the world, you may have to fake it a little, but not for long. You will soon not only play the confidence role, you'll feel it. If you recognize the qualities and talents you possess, the world will too. And when you can like yourself, you won't need anyone else's approval. You're talented, intelligent, healthy and attractive.

Now use it to your advantage.

AFTERTHOUGHTS

This "How-to" book is the result of many years of personal experience. I haven't always been an adulteress; for years I was a faithful wife who had tried most of the other solutions to "The Bored Housewife Syndrome." However, for me playing "The Game" seems to be the most fulfilling.

But I am not advocating that every bored housewife in America try it! This game is definitely not for everyone—but for those of you who do decide to play, this book will help you play sensibly, without peril, without complications. I've told it like it is; may you benefit from my experience.

My advice to would-be players is: Take adultery for what it is—a game and an alternative to divorce. If you play by the rules set forth in this book, you can't go wrong.

Hey—I've got to stop. Time has slipped by on me again. I've got just one hour until I see "him." And I don't mean my husband either! He's been fed and fussed over and is now napping peacefully in front of the TV. The children are all tucked in and sleeping, and I'm off to a rug-braiding class. Except tonight I'm skipping class—I have something *much* more interesting to do! Well, what are you waiting for? "The Game" could be just the answer for you too.